THE ORDER
OF MALTA

MINUTES WITH
THE CATECHISM

A Pocket Guide to the
Catechism of the Catholic Church

Peggy Stanton, DM

Foreword by Cardinal Timothy Dolan

Available from:
Marian Helpers Center
Stockbridge, MA 01263

Prayerline: 1-800-804-3823
Orderline: 1-800-462-7426

Websites:
Marian.org
ShopMercy.org

Library of Congress Control Number: 2023905383
ISBN: 978-1-59614-593-1

Imprimi Potest:
Very Rev. Chris Alar, MIC
Provincial Superior
The Blessed Virgin Mary, Mother of Mercy Province
March 20, 2023
Solemnity of St. Joseph

Nihil Obstat:
Robert A. Stackpole, STD
Censor Deputatus
March 20, 2023

Excerpts from the English translation of the *Catechism of the Catholic Church* for use in the United States of America Copyright © 1994, United States Catholic Conference, Inc. — Libreria Editrice Vaticana. Used with Permission. English translation of the *Catechism of the Catholic Church*: Modifications from the Editio Typica copyright © 1997, United States Conference of Catholic Bishops — Libreria Editrice Vaticana.

MARIAN PRESS
STOCKBRIDGE   MA 01263

Dedication

For the late Peter Muratore,
under whose direction
the "Malta Minutes" were born.

A catechism should faithfully and systematically present the teaching of Sacred Scripture, the living Tradition of the Church, and the authentic Magisterium, as well as the spiritual heritage of the Fathers and the Church's saints, to allow for a better knowledge of the Christian mystery and for enlivening the faith of the People of God. It should take into account the doctrinal statements which down the centuries the Holy Spirit has intimated to His Church. It should also help illumine with the light of faith the new situations and problems which had not yet emerged in the past. ...

In reading the *Catechism of the Catholic Church,* we can perceive the wondrous unity of the mystery of God, His saving will, as well as the central place of Jesus Christ, the only-begotten Son of God, sent by the Father, made Man in the womb of the Blessed Virgin Mary by the power of the Holy Spirit, to be our Savior. Having died and risen, Christ is always present in His Church, especially in the Sacraments; He is the source of our faith, the model of Christian conduct, and the Teacher of our prayer.

— **Pope St. John Paul II**,
Fidei Depositum, on the promulgation of the *Catechism of the Catholic Church*, October 11, 1992

Table of Contents

FOREWORD

What is the key to our spiritual growth? A faithful, personal, loving relationship with Jesus. To know Jesus, to hear Jesus, to love Jesus, to trust Jesus, to obey Jesus, to share His life in the deepest fiber of our being, to serve Him in this life – and then to share all eternity with Him in Heaven — this is our goal.

How do we achieve this, and grow in holiness? The best way is by a spiritual regimen that is both vigorous and multifaceted. If you were to ask some of the recent towering figures of our faith, like Pope Saint John Paul II or Saint Teresa of Calcutta, how best to follow Jesus, I suspect they'd suggest daily personal prayer, including daily Mass and reception of the Eucharist; fidelity to the Liturgy of the Hours, the ancient prayer of the Church that is encouraged for all, not just those in Holy Orders; spiritual direction, to promote integration and interiorization; frequent participation in the Sacrament of Penance; regular acts of charity and almsgiving for our brothers and sisters in need; a tireless effort to grow in virtue and turn away from sin. These should all be part of the pattern of our daily lives, with devotion to the Blessed Mother and the Saints as our examples and helpers.

Lastly, spiritual reading is a must. And here's where the *Catechism of the Catholic Church* plays a huge role.

Think of the *Catechism* as the how-to reference book for our Catholic faith. Everything you need to know, from the meaning of prayer, the Ten

Commandments, and the Sacraments to the role of the laity and the Church in the world — and so much more — is chronicled in beautiful, clear prose. But it's a big thick book, and I know that many Catholics find it intimidating.

God bless the Order of Malta American Association and my good friend, Peggy Stanton. For more than a decade, "The Order of Malta Minute with the *Catechism*" has introduced millions of listeners to the richness and usefulness of the *Catechism*. Broadcast daily by Peggy on Ave Maria Radio and other radio networks, the Minutes have become tremendously popular across the country.

I'm delighted that Peggy's scripts are now published, with handy reference numbers for future reading. My hope is that this practical book will become a daily devotional and inspiration, encouraging readers from the Order of Malta and beyond to crack open the big book.

That we may be good, holy, happy, healthy, learned, zealous, selfless, committed faithful is the goal of our spiritual growth. The pages that follow — a veritable road map to the *Catechism* — are a good place to begin.

— **His Eminence, Timothy Cardinal Dolan,**
Archbishop of New York
Principal Chaplain,
Order of Malta American Association

INTRODUCTION

They were not meant for broadcast. Or so I thought. The "Order of Malta Minute with the *Catechism*" evolved out of the ether.

The Order of Malta American Association had been communicating "minutes" on the air for perhaps a year or more as a spiritual outreach. They were brief, inspiring stories written by a priest. I was asked as a former broadcaster to voice them. Which I did.

Eventually the priest ran out of stories, but the Order had not run out of the desire to communicate spiritual outreach on the air. Peter Muratore, chairman of the Communications Committee on which I served, asked me for ideas as to new Minute content. For years, I had been urging we do something with the *Catechism of the Catholic Church*. Eventually a half-hour television show was produced, but nothing on a continuing basis.

So, feeling spiritually nudged, I began reading the *Catechism* from beginning to end, every morning, usually just a subject per day and then writing a meditation, highlighting the most memorable points. When Peter queried me as to what evangelical content the Order could broadcast, once again, I proposed the *Catechism*.

Necessity is the mother of acceptance. This time the *Catechism* got the green light. At that time, my little meditations numbered over 150. When I read them out loud, they all timed between 50 to 60 seconds: perfect size for a one-minute broadcast!

"What would we call them?" Peter wanted to know.

"The Order of Malta Minute with the *Catechism*," I replied.

To make sure I hadn't committed heresy paring doctrine down to almost text-sized explanations, Peter wisely insisted that the "Malta Minutes" be vetted by knowledgeable clergy. We enlisted the aid of Msgr. Douglas Mathers, a canon lawyer, to review 10 at a time before I recorded them. Monsignor, who is a busy pastor of a Manhattan parish, carefully examined each for accuracy. A discussion on the telephone followed. Sometimes the corrections, if they were necessary, involved only a word, but a word can make a big difference when disclosing doctrine.

Those telephone conferences with Msgr. Mathers, who is a delightful man as well as extremely intelligent, were the highlights of producing the "Malta Minutes" for me. Another highlight was working with Ave Maria Radio, where the "Malta Minutes" were recorded, sponsored by the Order of Malta. Mike Jones, general manager, and Al Kresta, chief executive officer, were gracious collaborators.

Steve Clarke, the chief engineer, who did the actual recordings, was wonderful to work with. I had not been on the air regularly for many years, and he was most gracious, waiting for me to get my elocution back up to one-minute speed.

* * * * *

The "Malta Minutes" were first broadcast in 2011 and have been on the air nationally ever since, sometimes four times a day. When listener requests came in to the network for copies of the scripts, we began talking about making them into a book. Not until Dr. Joe McAleer, my splendid editor at Marian Press, suggested that I do a book on the *Catechism* did the talk turn into action. The fact that there were already more than 250 "Malta Minute" scripts in existence lightened the load of the project.

"The Order of Malta Minute with the *Catechism*" has reached a much wider and more enthusiastic audience than I ever anticipated, but it confirmed my original conviction of the importance of the *Catechism*. The people in the pews hunger for knowledge of their faith, to know how to respond when questioned *why* you believe *what* you believe.

The *Catechism* is divided into four sections: the Profession of Faith, the Celebration of the Christian Mystery, Life in Christ, and Christian Prayer. As Pope St. John Paul II explained in his 1992 Apostolic Constitution, *Fidei Depositum* (The Deposit of Faith), on the publication of the *Catechism*:

> The four parts are related one to the other: the Christian mystery is the object of faith (first part); it is celebrated and communicated in liturgical actions (second part); it is present to enlighten and sustain the children of God in their actions (third part); it is the basis for our prayer, the privileged expression of which

is the *Our Father*, and it represents the object of our supplication, our praise and our intercession (fourth part).[1]

Given the length and breadth of the *Catechism*, the "Malta Minutes" that follow are merely a taste — condensed teachings from each of the four parts that distill the essentials of doctrine in the *Catechism*.

My fervent hope is that, as you read each "Malta Minute," you will be inspired to pick up the *Catechism* and read more about the topic, using the handy reference numbers provided. In the full *Catechism* the richness of our Catholic faith will unfold before you.

— **Peggy Stanton, DM**

---

[1] Pope John Paul II, *Fidei Depositum*, October 11, 1992, vatican.va/content/john-paul-ii/en/apost_constitutions/documents/hf_jp-ii_apc_19921011_fidei-depositum.html

PART ONE:

THE PROFESSION
OF FAITH

God's Valentine

Do you know the origin of the rainbow? While the *Catechism* gives the reasoning and the implications of the covenant between God and Noah after the Flood, it points us to the Bible and Genesis 9:12–17 for the romantic story of the sign God promised He would give to remind Himself and mankind of that covenant:

> God said: This is the sign of the covenant that I am making between me and you and every living creature with you for all ages to come. I set my bow in the clouds to serve as a sign of the covenant between me and the earth. When I bring clouds over the earth, and the bow appears in the clouds, I will remember my covenant between me and you and every living creature — every mortal being — so that the waters will never again become a flood to destroy every mortal being. When the bow appears in the clouds, I will see it and remember the everlasting covenant between God and every living creature — every mortal being that is on earth. God told Noah: This is the sign of the covenant I have established between me and every mortal being that is on earth.

Little wonder such a vivid valentine from our Creator excites our eyes.

The Holy Spirit,
One with the Father and the Son

Para. 243–245, 689, 809

From whom does the Holy Spirit come?

Jesus promises the Holy Spirit, says the *Catechism*, when the time of His glorification arrives. In answer to Jesus' prayers, the Father sends, in Jesus' Name, "another Paraclete" or Advocate, the Holy Spirit of truth. The Father sends Him in Jesus' Name, and Jesus sends Him from His place at His Father's side, since He comes from the Father.

The Holy Spirit will remain with us forever. He will teach us everything, remind us what Christ said, and bear witness to Christ.

When Jesus delivered the Spirit by breathing on the apostles, His combined mission with the Spirit became the mission of the Church. The Church is the temple of the Holy Spirit: the Spirit, as it were, of the mystical body, the source of its life, of its unity in diversity, and of the riches of His gifts and charisms.

Made in the
Image and Likeness of God
Para. 355–358

What does it actually mean that man is made in the image and likeness of God? It means that man is unique in God's world, according to the *Catechism*.

In his own nature, man unites the spiritual and material world. God created them male and female, Scripture tells us. Only man, of all God's creatures, is able to know and love God. He is the only creature willed into existence for his own sake.

Man is not just *something*. He is *some one*, capable of self-knowledge and self-possession. He is able to be freely in communication with other men and women, and he is called to a covenant with his Creator. "He alone, is called to share," says the *Catechism*, "by knowledge and love, in God's own life. It was for this that he was created, and this is the fundamental reason for his dignity."

Men and women are asked to respond to God with love and faith in a way that no other creatures can. The *Catechism* states, "God created everything for man, but man in turn was created to serve and love God and to offer all creation back to him."

What Exactly is the Soul?

Para. 362–366

What exactly is the soul? It is what makes a person a living being. Scripture tells us in Genesis 2:7, when God created Adam, He formed him from the dust of the Earth, "and breathed into his nostrils the breath of life, and man became a living being."

The soul is the innermost aspect of man, the *Catechism* states, "that which is of greatest value in him, that by which he is most especially in God's image: 'soul' signifies the *spiritual principle* in man."

The human body is animated by the soul. At no time is this more evident than at the moment of death, when the soul leaves the body and the observer can clearly see the life drained out of it as the body becomes totally still, loses color, and loses all vitality and personality that was once within it. The soul carries all these qualities with it into eternity and will return them to the body when the two are rejoined at the final resurrection.

The Big Bad Guy of the Universe

Para. 391–395

Who is the big bad guy of the universe? "Behind the disobedient choice of our first parents," reveals the *Catechism*, "lurks a seductive voice, opposed to God, which makes them fall into death out of envy." Church tradition and Scripture identify this evil being as Satan or the "devil."

Satan and his minions, all created spirits — angels — were originally designed as good by God, but became evil by their own doing, making a free and radical choice to reject God and His reign. "It is the *irrevocable* character of their choice," says the *Catechism*, "and not a defect in the infinite divine mercy, that makes the angels' sin unforgivable. 'There is no repentance for the angels after their fall, just as there is no repentance for men after death.'"

Jesus labeled Satan a "murderer from the beginning." The reason Jesus appeared in human history was to destroy the works of the devil. As powerful as the devil is, his power is finite. He is only a creature up against the Creator, whose power is infinite.

Exile from Eden Leads to Rescue by a Divine Redeemer

Para. 402–406

What was the sin that exiled man from the Garden of Eden? It was the sin of disobedience, according to the *Catechism*. And it was Jesus' obedience to the Father that reopened the possibility of Paradise to the human race. He took on our sins — He who never sinned — in order to expiate our offenses.

No mere human, however holy, could achieve such a feat. Christ's divinity alongside His humanity made him unique. Thus He was the only Savior able to reconcile the world to God because He was God.

In taking on a human nature, Jesus opened the avenue for us to partner with Him in the Paschal Mystery. He asks His disciples to take up their own crosses and follow His example by offering our sufferings up as expiation for sin, thus giving redeeming merit to misery.

Why Did the Word Become Flesh?

Para. 456–460

The Word became flesh to redeem us from our sinful state, the *Catechism* tells us, and reconcile us to God. We lived in darkness and needed a great light. We were prisoners and needed to be freed. In such a miserable state, we needed a divine/human mediator to descend from Heaven.

Through Jesus' suffering and death, we learned how much God loved us: "For God so loved the world that he gave his only Son, that whoever believes in him should not perish but have eternal life." For divinity to descend to humanity, and humanity in the poorest circumstances, demanded great love, great sacrifice, and great humility. It also gave us a great role model whom we could and should imitate on our life's journey.

Jesus is the embodiment of the Beatitudes and the norm of the New Law. He commanded us to "love one another as I have loved you."

Was Mary Truly a Virgin?

Para. 496–501

Has the Church always professed the virginity of Jesus' mother, Mary? Yes, says the *Catechism*. From the very beginning, the Church has always maintained that Jesus came into the womb of the Blessed Mother solely by the power of the Holy Spirit, seeing in the virginal conception the sign that it truly was the Son of God who came in a humanity like our own.

The Gospels all make it clear that the virginal conception was something beyond human comprehension; a divine work as prophesied in Isaiah: "Behold, a virgin shall conceive and bear a son." Mary, according to the *Catechism*, remained a virgin her entire life. Jesus was her only physical Son, "but her spiritual motherhood extends to all men whom indeed he came to save."

Why Does the Bible Refer to Jesus' Brothers and Sisters?

Para. 500–501

If Jesus' Mother, Mary, was always a virgin, why does the Bible refer to Jesus' "brothers and sisters"? The *Catechism* explains it thus: "The Church has always understood these passages as not referring to other children of the Virgin Mary."

The Old Testament expression "brothers and sisters" could mean close relations, not necessarily siblings. In fact, it is pointed out, James and John, referred to as "brothers of Jesus," are the sons of another Mary, a disciple of Christ who St. Matthew in his Gospel significantly calls "the other Mary."

The *Catechism* states, "Jesus is Mary's only son, but her spiritual motherhood extends to all men whom indeed he came to save."

Mystery Is Love of God

Para. 514–518

Ever wonder why we are all fascinated with mystery? Perhaps it is because our Creator God *is* mystery. From His amazing birth from a virgin to His equally amazing death and Resurrection, God's entire existence on earth in Jesus Christ is mystery.

The *Catechism* tells us that, in Christ, the whole fullness of Deity dwelled bodily. "What was visible in his earthly life," says the *Catechism*, "leads to the invisible mystery of his divine sonship and redemptive mission."

Christ's earthly journey also serves as a revelation of the Father. "Whoever has seen me has seen the Father," Jesus said. He became Man to do His Father's will.

"Because our Lord became man in order to do his Father's will," the *Catechism* says, "even the least characteristics of his mysteries manifest 'God's love ... among us.' Christ's whole life is a mystery of redemption."

All of Christ's Life, Hidden and Public, Is for Our Redemption

Para. 516–518

There is so much emphasis on Christ's death and Resurrection that we do not focus enough on all His 33 years on the earth. The *Catechism* tells us that, all during those years, Jesus was, in effect, redeeming us.

Through His Incarnation, He enriches us by His poverty. In His hidden years, His voluntary obedience to Mary and Joseph atones for our disobedience. His word purifies His listeners. In His miracles of healing and His casting out of evil spirits, He took on our infirmities and bore our diseases.

Finally, in His Resurrection, He justified us. The *Catechism* states that "All Jesus did, said, and suffered had for its aim restoring fallen man to his original vocation ... being in the image and likeness of God."

Jesus' life on earth gave us a shortcut to salvation.

What Events of Jesus' Infancy Reveal

What do the revealed events of Jesus' infancy signify? According to the *Catechism*, Jesus' circumcision signals His incorporation into the people of the covenant, Abraham's descendants.

The Epiphany portrays Jesus as the Messiah, the Savior of all people. The Magi arriving from different lands indicate that the Gospel will spread to all peoples, but that they must turn toward the Jews and the Messianic message contained in the Old Testament.

The Presentation in the Temple reveals Jesus to be the firstborn Son who belongs to the Lord. Simeon's prediction of a sword that will pierce Mary's heart is a prophecy of the oblation of the Cross.

The flight into Egypt and the slaughter of the innocents display the opposition of darkness to the light.

The Salvific Significance
of Jesus' Hidden Life

What is the value of Jesus' hidden life in Nazareth? The *Catechism* points out, "During the greater part of his life Jesus shared the condition of the vast majority of human beings: a daily life spent without evident greatness, a life of manual labor" as a carpenter.

Jesus' obedience to His earthly parents fulfills the Fourth Commandment perfectly and forms a temporal image of His obedience to His heavenly Father. Through this obedience, He already began His work of restoring the damage done by Adam's disobedience.

This humble period also binds us to Jesus in the ordinary events of our lives. The "school of Nazareth" teaches us three things: the value of silence, the value of family life, and the value of work.

The Drama at the Jordan

Can you imagine the scene at the river Jordan when Jesus was baptized? Here is John the Baptist baptizing a whole crowd of sinners, and suddenly, there in the midst of them, stands the Sinless One. John hesitates, but Jesus insists. The Holy Spirit in the form of a dove comes to rest over Jesus' Head, and the voice of the Father is heard from the heavens, proclaiming, "This is my beloved Son."

The *Catechism* says, "The baptism of Jesus is on his part the acceptance and inauguration of his mission as God's suffering Servant." Jesus accepts the Baptism and the mission that will culminate on the Cross. "At his baptism 'the heavens were opened' — the heavens that Adam's sin had closed — and the waters were sanctified by the descent of Jesus and the Spirit, a prelude to the new creation," the *Catechism* states.

Christ is the second Adam.

Vanquishing the Tempter

Why would God permit the devil to tempt His Son in the desert? The symbolism behind those temptations, as provided by the *Catechism*, gives great insight into God's rationale.

Jesus, driven by the Spirit, goes into the desert to live in solitude for 40 days. At the close of that period of prayer and fasting, the devil arrives to attempt to compromise Jesus' filial devotion to God, His Father. Satan tempts Jesus three times and Jesus rebuffs him three times. This is a recapitulation of Satan's temptations of Adam in Paradise — only this time, he loses to the "second Adam." It is also a recapitulation of Israel in the desert when the Hebrews provoked God during their 40-year sojourn. In contrast, Jesus is totally obedient to His Father's will.

Jesus' victory over temptation is a prelude to His victory over sin on the Cross.

How the Creator Can Relate to His Creatures

Para. 540–542

How do Jesus's temptations in the desert help Him relate to us? According to the *Catechism*, the fact that Jesus is tested in every way we are makes Him a high priest who is able to sympathize with our weaknesses: "By the solemn forty days of *Lent* the Church unites herself each year to the mystery of Jesus in the desert."

After John the Baptist is arrested, Jesus comes to Galilee, exhorting His listeners to repent, for the Kingdom of God is at hand. To carry out the will of the Father, which is to lift up men to share in His divine life, Jesus invites all people to gather around Him. That gathering is the Church on earth, the seed and beginning of the Kingdom.

It is through the Paschal Mystery that Jesus accomplishes the coming of the Kingdom.

Proclaiming the Kingdom
Para. 543–546

Whom does Jesus invite to enter the Kingdom of Heaven? The *Catechism* tells us He invites all to enter. Originally announced to the Israelites, the Kingdom is now open to people of every nation. But to enter that Kingdom, one must accept Jesus' word.

The Kingdom belongs to the poor and lowly with whom Jesus identifies. The "poor and lowly" means those who have accepted the Kingdom with humble hearts. To the "little ones," the Father is pleased to reveal what is hidden from the wise and the learned. Jesus makes active love toward the poor of every kind a condition for entering the Kingdom.

Jesus invites sinners into the Kingdom and speaks of the joy in Heaven over the repentance of just one sinner. Jesus' invitation to the Kingdom comes in the form of parables.

To enter the Kingdom, mere words are not enough, however. Deeds are also demanded. One must give everything.

Miracles: Signs of the Kingdom

Para. 547–550

What evidence did Jesus give that He was indeed the Messiah? Keeping company with His words, Jesus performed many miracles, attesting to the fact that He was indeed the One sent by the Father.

When people turned to Jesus in faith, He granted what they asked, curing many diseases, restoring sight to the blind and hearing to the deaf.

Despite these wonders, some people still rejected Jesus. Though the Lord released many from physical sufferings, He did not come to abolish all evils from the earth, but to free mankind from the severest form of slavery: sin, which, the *Catechism* states, "thwarts them in their vocation as God's sons and causes all forms of human bondage."

Defeating Satan's Kingdom

Para. 547–553

How does the defeat of Satan's kingdom come about? The *Catechism* tells us that defeat comes about through the Cross of Christ, which establishes the Kingdom of God.

The exorcisms Jesus performed to free individuals from demonic domination point to Jesus' great victory over the "ruler of the world." The *Catechism* points out, "'God reigned from the wood,'" the Cross.

At the very start of His mission, Jesus chose 12 men to accompany Him and to participate in the mission. The choice was made for all time. Through them, says the *Catechism*, Jesus directs the Church. "As my Father appointed a kingdom for me, so do I appoint you," Jesus told the apostles.

Jesus entrusted a unique mission to Peter after Peter professed to Him, "You are the Christ, the Son of the Living God." Jesus then created the first pope. "Thou art Peter and on this Rock," He said, "I will build my Church."

Jesus Revealed:
The Transfiguration

Para. 554–556

When and how did Jesus allow some of His apostles to see Him in His glory? After entrusting to Peter the keys to govern the house of God — the Church — the Lord began to reveal to His followers that He must go to Jerusalem and suffer many things, including death, but that, on the third day, He would be raised from that death.

It is during this period, according to the *Catechism*, that He takes Peter, James, and John up on a high mountain and there unveils His divine glory for a very brief time. His clothing, His face, become dazzling with light. He also reveals that He must go by way of the Cross in Jerusalem to enter His glory.

All the Trinity is present for the Transfiguration; the Father in the voice declaring Jesus to be His beloved Son; the Son in Jesus; the Spirit in the cloud that covers Jesus.

The Transfiguration gives us a window on Jesus' glorious coming and our own transformation from a lowly body to a glorious body like His. The *Catechism* reminds us, however, that "'it is through many persecutions that we must enter the kingdom of God.'" It is called following in the footsteps of the Master.

Jesus and the Rivaling Rabbis

Para. 581–582

How was Jesus seen by the Jews of His day? He was viewed as a rabbi by the Jewish people and their spiritual leaders, according to the *Catechism*. Nevertheless, "Jesus could not help but offend teachers of the Law, for he was not content to propose his interpretation alongside theirs," but taught the people with divine authority, and the people recognized the superiority of His teaching about the law.

Jesus did not abolish the law. He fulfilled it and gave its ultimate interpretation in a divine way. Jesus even interpreted the dietary laws that the Jews held so dear. He declared all foods "clean" when He said it was not what goes into a man that defiles him, but what comes out of him, such as evil thoughts.

Certain teachers confronted Jesus because they did not agree with His interpretations despite the miracles that accompanied His teaching and pointed to His divinity.

Jesus' Reverence for the Temple

Para. 583–586

Jesus had great respect for the temple in Jerusalem, according to the *Catechism*. It was the special dwelling of His Father where He could go and commune with Him.

Though He was God Himself, He was perfectly willing to pay the Temple tax, and yet He foretold the destruction of the Temple, a time when "there would not remain a stone upon a stone." Jesus — who was the ultimate dwelling place, the bodily temple of God — would, the *Catechism* says, "manifest the dawning of a new age in the history of salvation."

The Lord declared, "The hour is coming when neither on this mountain nor in Jerusalem will you worship the Father."

Recognizing Jesus
Para. 587–591

The greatest stumbling block Jesus presented to certain of the religious authorities of His day was His relationship with sinners. He ate with them. He commingled with them just as He did with the religious authorities, as if the sinners were as good as the religious authorities, which the latter thought impossible.

Jesus reminded the authorities, "I have not come to call the righteous, but sinners to repentance." He also reminded them, the *Catechism* states, "that, since sin is universal, those who pretend not to need salvation are blind to themselves" and only fooling themselves.

The final blow was Jesus forgiving sins, which the authorities thought only God could do. They were right in this assumption, but wrong in refusing to recognize that Jesus *was* God.

The Trial of Jesus

Who is responsible for the death of Jesus? The *Catechism* emphatically states that neither the Jews of Jesus' time nor the Jews of our time should be considered rejected or accursed as a consequence of the Lord's Passion.

Not all the Jews in the religious hierarchy were opposed to Jesus. Nicodemus and Joseph of Arimathea were two prominent men who were secret disciples. The Acts of the Apostles notes that many priests were obedient to the faith, and some belonged to the party of the Pharisees. Saint James reported to St. Paul that many thousands believed in the Lord and were also "zealous for the Law."

The religious authorities were not in unanimity as to what to do with Jesus. The Pharisees threatened excommunication to His followers. The Sanhedrin, having declared Him a blasphemer but without power to execute, turned Him over to the Romans as a political anarchist.

Because of all the historical complexity concerning Jesus' trial and the Jews, the *Catechism* cautions we must leave judgment as to the participants to God alone.

We Are All to Blame

Just who is to blame for Jesus' Crucifixion? The Church blames you, me, and all sinners, for the suffering of the Savior, says the *Catechism*.

We would like to heap all the blame on the Jews of Jesus' era and forget our own guilt, but the Church will not allow it. We are reminded that Christ came to save all sinners through all ages.

Moreover, the Church points out that our responsibility is even greater than the Jews of Jesus' day. We *know* who Jesus is. Many of them did not. They acted out of ignorance. "We must regard as guilty all those who continue to relapse into their sins," the *Catechism* states, "since our sins made the Lord Christ suffer the torment of the cross."

Every time we sin now, we wound the Lord again in our hearts, which is where He lives: an awesome and sorrowful thought.

Who Took Jesus' Life?

Who took Jesus' life? No one took Jesus' life, according to the *Catechism*. Jesus freely gave up His life and took it up again. He knew His Passion and death were the instruments of His Father's redemptive plan —that this was His Father's desire, and thus it was His desire.

At the Last Supper, Jesus made a memorial of His voluntary offering to His Father when He instituted the Eucharist. He made the apostles the priests of the New Covenant when He told them to perpetuate the memorial.

The *Catechism* tells us, "In suffering and death his humanity became the free and perfect instrument of his divine love which desires the salvation of men."

To Do the Will of the Father

Para. 606–609

Why did the Second Person of the Blessed Trinity leave His magnificent residence in Heaven at the right hand of the Father? To do the will of the Father, the *Catechism* tells us.

Jesus assumed flesh and blood, voluntarily joining His divinity to humanity to accomplish His mission, and that mission was to "serve and give his life as a ransom for many," says the *Catechism*. Such was His sustenance. "My food," Jesus proclaimed, "is to do the will of Him who sent me."

Jesus disdained any suggestion that He abandon the dual role of Paschal Lamb and Suffering Servant who "silently allows himself to be led to the slaughter," as the *Catechism* phrases it.

"Shall I not," Jesus asks, "drink the cup the Father has given me?"

Why Did God Do It?

Para. 613–615

Why did God the Father permit His only Son to endure such torture, humiliation, and death for such an unworthy and ungrateful group as we humans? It is probably the greatest mystery of all time. The only explanations are love and justice, the *Catechism* tells us.

The Father so loved His creatures that He gave up His only Son to the Cross to redeem us and to reconcile us to Himself. The Son loved us enough to freely offer up His life to the Father as a redemptive and reconciling act, making Him both the Paschal Sacrifice — "'the Lamb of God, who takes away the sin of the world'" — and the *"sacrifice of the New Covenant,* which restores man to communion with God."

Justice enters the scene because man's disobedience required a monumental and unique sacrifice that only the Son of God made Man could achieve.

Christ's Death and Burial

Para. 624–626

What took place between Christ's Crucifixion and His Resurrection? The *Catechism* calls that period "the mystery of the tomb."

Christ truly died. His human Soul and Body were separated from one another as His Body lay in the tomb. But His Divine Person retained possession of both. Divine power preserved His Body from corruption, though His death on the Cross ended His earthly existence.

Thus Christ, by the grace of God, actually tasted death for everyone.

"Christ's stay in the tomb," the *Catechism* states, "constitutes the real link between his passible state before Easter and his glorious and risen state today. The same person of the 'Living One' can say, 'I died, and behold I am alive for evermore.'"

In that one Person, the *Catechism* states, is "*the meeting point for death and life.*"

He Descended into Hell

Why would Jesus do such a thing? How often when we recite the Apostles' Creed and utter the phrase "He descended into hell," we struggle with the idea of Jesus Christ mingling with demons.

In fact, Jesus did not descend into the hell of damnation. He went down into the bowels of the earth (figuratively speaking) to free the souls of the just who had died before His Passion and Resurrection.

The *Catechism* quotes an ancient Holy Saturday homily that depicts the Lord searching for Adam and Eve to free them from their sorrow and bondage. When Jesus died, His soul joined the realm of the dead, in order to announce to those who had gone before the Good News that Jesus, "'the Author of Life,' by dying destroyed 'him who has the power of death, that is, the devil, and [delivered] all those who through fear of death were subject to lifelong bondage.'"

Witnesses to the Resurrection
Para. 640–644

Who were the first people to view the Risen Christ? They were Mary Magdalene and the women who came to finish anointing His Body, a process that had been discontinued when the Sabbath began on the evening of Good Friday. Thus, it is significant to note, as the *Catechism* does, that "women were the first messengers of Christ's Resurrection for the apostles themselves."

The women informed the apostles who were the next to see Jesus: Peter first, because his testimony strengthened the faith of his companions.

The apostles' faith was severely tested by the death of Christ — so much so that they were not easily convinced by the women's report. Even after seeing Jesus, some apostles thought the apparition was a ghost. Thus, for some to claim the Resurrection was a fable created by the Christian community does not hold up.

Jesus' Risen Body

Para. 645–646

Was Jesus' Risen Body the same Body He dwelled in while living on earth? According to the *Catechism*, it was the same Body that was crucified, but it was glorified and different in profound ways from the risen body of Lazarus, whom Jesus brought forth from the tomb.

Lazarus returned to his same earthly life with the same limitations he had when he left it. "Christ's Resurrection is essentially different," asserts the *Catechism*. "In his risen body he passes from the state of death to another life beyond time and space."

Jesus rose with new powers. He could appear and disappear at will. He could walk through doors. He could also eat and drink as He did with the apostles to prove to them that He was not a ghost. He could appear in whatever guise He chose, as He did with Mary Magdalene when she thought He was the gardener.

"At Jesus' Resurrection," the *Catechism* says, "his body is filled with the power of the Holy Spirit: he shares the divine life in his glorious state, so that St. Paul can say that Christ is 'the man of heaven.'"

The Mysteries of the Resurrection

What is the great mystery of the Christian faith? It is, of course, the Resurrection of Jesus Christ, even though the Resurrection is a historical fact professed by the apostles and signified by the empty tomb.

No one knows the exact hour Jesus emerged from the tomb. There were no eyewitnesses to describe the actual moment; only the result: the live appearances of Jesus to His disciples. It is an event that "transcends and surpasses history," the *Catechism* tells us.

The three Persons of the Trinity, using their individual characteristics, acted as one in bringing about the Resurrection. God the Father raised up the Son. God the Holy Spirit "gave life to Jesus' dead humanity and called it to the glorious state of Lordship." The Son "effects his own Resurrection by virtue of his divine power." He predicted the Passion and declared that He had the power to lay down His life and to take it up again.

Jesus' Ascension into Heaven

Para. 659–664

When Jesus disappeared into the clouds, leaving His apostles behind, where did He go? According to the *Catechism*, He went to Heaven to take His place at the right hand of the Father. Just as He descended from Heaven at the moment of the Incarnation, at the Ascension, He returned to the Father, something only He, the God-Man, the Son of the Father, could do.

Thus the Incarnation and the Ascension are inextricably linked. "Only the one who 'came from the Father' can return to the Father," the *Catechism* tells us, further stating that the Ascension of the Lord introduces the irreversible entry of His humanity into divine glory where He will be seated from this time forward at God's right hand.

Left to our own devices, we mortals could not achieve access to Heaven. We are totally dependent on the merits gained for us by the One who went before us.

When Will Christ Return?

Para. 668–675

Christ is already present here in His Church, according to the *Catechism*, but His glorious messianic reign as predicted by the prophets will not come about until all things are subject to Him, and then men and women will live in peace and justice.

Before that glorious reign, however, the Church must pass through a great trial that will shake the faith of many believers: the appearance of the Antichrist, when truth will be sacrificed to apostasy.

The present time is a time of Spirit and witness, but also a time of great distress — a "trial of evil which does not spare the Church and ushers in the struggles of the last days," says the *Catechism*. "It is a time of waiting and watching."

Jesus Comes to Judge the Living and the Dead

Para. 678–679

What will happen when Jesus Christ comes to judge the living and the dead? On the last day, the *Catechism* tells us, everything will be laid bare: the deeds, thoughts, and works of all men and women. Then will "culpable unbelief" be condemned. Culpable unbelief discounts the offer of God's grace as nothing.

Our attitude toward our neighbor will reveal our acceptance or rejection of God's grace and divine love. Our Lord will say, "Truly, I say to you, as you did it to one of the least of these my brethren, you did it to me."

Though Christ is given authority over all judgment — a right He "'acquired'" by way of the Cross as Redeemer of the world, the *Catechism* reminds us — Jesus did not come to judge but to save and to give the life He has within Himself.

If we reject the grace we receive in this life, we already judge ourselves, according to our works. We can even condemn ourselves for all eternity by rejecting the Spirit of Love.

Visible Signs of the Holy Spirit in the Church

Para. 687–690

How is the Holy Spirit evident in the Church? In many ways, says the *Catechism*:

- Through the Scriptures He inspired;
- in Tradition;
- in the Church's Magisterium, which He assists;
- in the Church's Sacramental Liturgy;
- in prayer, where He intercedes for us;
- in the Church's charisms and ministries;
- in the signs of her apostolic and ministerial life;
- and in the witness of the Saints.

The Holy Spirit is the Spirit of the Son and is truly God, consubstantial with the Father and the Son and, according to the *Catechism*, "inseparable from them, in both the inner life of the Trinity and his gift of love for the world."

The Son and the Spirit have a joint mission. The Son is the visible image of the Invisible God, but, says the *Catechism*, "it is the Spirit who reveals him."

Names for the Holy Spirit

What is the proper name for the third person of the Blessed Trinity? The *Catechism* tells us that the proper name is the Holy Spirit, a name the Church received from the second person of the Blessed Trinity.

The term "Spirit" from the Hebrew word *ruah* means "breath, air, wind," but, when joined with the word "Holy," clearly designates the third person of the Trinity.

Jesus, in promising to send the Holy Spirit, calls Him the "Paraclete," which means he who is called to one's side. Another translation is the "Consoler." Jesus also referred to the Holy Spirit as the "Spirit of Truth."

Saint Paul used many titles: "Spirit of the Promise," "Spirit of Adoption," "Spirit of Christ," "Spirit of the Lord," and "Spirit of God."

Saint Peter called Him the Spirit of Glory.

John the Baptist

Para. 717–720

In a sense, John the Baptist is the mouthpiece of the Holy Spirit. He was filled with the Spirit even before his birth, when Elizabeth reported to Mary that the babe in her womb leaped for joy as Mary arrived, pregnant with Jesus, to visit and assist her cousin.

John the Baptist was the Elijah promised to come before the arrival of the Messiah. He also completes the cycle of prophets that began with Elijah.

In John, the *Catechism* tells us, "The Holy Spirit begins the restoration to man of 'the divine likeness,' prefiguring what he would achieve with and in Christ."

Mary: God's Masterpiece

Para. 721–726

Who is the Creator's masterpiece? The *Catechism* says that God's masterwork of the mission of the Son and the Spirit is the all-holy, ever Virgin Mary. She, for the first time, was the dwelling where the Father could place His Son and His Spirit to live among men.

The Church, says the *Catechism*, has often read the most beautiful texts on wisdom as relating to Mary. She is acclaimed in liturgy as the "Seat of Wisdom."

The Holy Spirit prepared Mary for her great task by filling her with grace, and by sheer grace she was conceived without sin. It was appropriate that she, in whom the Eternal Son would dwell, would herself be without any stain of original sin.

The Arrival of the Holy Spirit

When did Jesus reveal the existence of the Holy Spirit? Though the Lord alluded to the Spirit in speaking to Nicodemus and to the Samaritan woman, the *Catechism* tells us, "Jesus does not reveal the Holy Spirit fully, until he himself has been glorified through his Death and Resurrection."

Little by little, nevertheless, Jesus did also refer to the Holy Spirit, even when teaching to the multitudes, as when He says His own flesh will be food for the life of the world. He spoke openly to his disciples about "the Spirit in connection with prayer and with the witness they will have to bear," the *Catechism* notes.

When the hour for His glorification arrives, Jesus actually promises the arrival of the Holy Spirit. "The Spirit of truth, the other Paraclete," says the *Catechism*, "will be given by the Father in answer to Jesus' prayer; he will be sent by the Father in Jesus' name."

Love, the First Gift

Para. 733–737

What is God's first gift to the Church? The *Catechism* proclaims, "'God is Love' and love is his first gift, containing all others."

The Holy Spirit, who has been given to us, pours God's love into us. The first effect of love is the forgiveness of sin. The communion of the Holy Spirit in the Church restores the Divine Likeness that was lost through sin. The Holy Spirit gives us the first fruits of our inheritance, the very life of the Holy Trinity. That fruit is to love, says the *Catechism*, as God has loved us.

The evidence, or fruits, of the Holy Spirit are love, joy, peace, patience, kindness, goodness, faithfulness, gentleness, and self-control. The more we renounce ourselves, the more we live by the Spirit.

The mission of Christ and the Holy Spirit are brought to completion in the Church.

The Holy Catholic Church
Para. 748–750

When the Second Vatican Council spoke about the Church, its opening words defined Christ as "the light of humanity." The Council further stated its desire, meeting together in the Holy Spirit, to "bring all men to the light of Christ by proclaiming his Gospel to every creature."

Christ's light is most visible in His Church. The holiness of the Church is from the source of all holiness, the Holy Spirit. The Holy Spirit is also the giver of all holiness. The Church, says the *Catechism*, is "the place 'where the Spirit flourishes.'"

Our belief in the Father, Son, and Holy Spirit cannot be separated from a belief that the Church is holy and Catholic, one and apostolic.

A Church of Many Names

Jesus said His Father's house had many mansions. He might have added the Church He founded has many names, such as "a cultivated field, the tillage of God."

The *Catechism* explains that the Church's holy "roots" were the prophets, and that the "land, like a choice vineyard, has been planted by the heavenly cultivator." The true vine is Christ, who gives life and fruit to us, the branches.

The Church is referred to as "our mother" and the "spotless spouse of the spotless lamb." Another name for the Church is the "*building* of God." The *Catechism* reminds us that Jesus compared Himself to the "stone which the builders rejected, but which was made into the cornerstone."

The Church is also called the "House of God," the "Holy Temple," the "Holy City," and the "New Jerusalem."

Jesus' Mission

Para. 763–766

What was Jesus' chief mission on earth? It was, the *Catechism* tells us, to achieve His Father's will, God's plan of salvation in the fullness of time. Jesus did this by preaching the Good News: the arrival of the reign of God, which had been promised through the ages in Scripture.

To fulfill the Father's will, Jesus ushered in the Kingdom of Heaven on earth. The Kingdom is visible in the word and worship of Christ and in His Presence in the Church.

The *Catechism* notes, "The seed and beginning of the Kingdom are the 'little flock' of those whom Jesus came to gather around him" — the disciples and the twelve apostles, with Peter as the head. They are the foundation stones of the New Jerusalem.

The Church is born primarily as a result of Christ's total self-giving. The origin and growth of the Church are symbolized by the blood and water that flowed from the crucified Christ's side.

Mystery of the Church
Para. 770–771

What is the dual role of the Catholic Church? The *Catechism* says the Church is in history and yet transcends history. Only the "'eyes of faith'" can discern her in her visible identity and at the same time see her spiritual reality as bearer of divine reality.

Christ, the one Mediator, established the Church and also sustains her on earth as a visible organization through which He communicates truth and grace to all mankind.

The Church is both a society structured with hierarchical organs and the Mystical Body of Christ: a visible society and a spiritual community. Saint Bernard of Clairvaux called the Church "both tabernacle of cedar and sanctuary of God; earthly dwelling and celestial palace."

The Church — The People of God

What does the *Catechism* call the Church? It calls it the People of God, and teaches that God willed to save man as "a people" with links to one another. For this reason, He chose the Israelites to be His people, and made a covenant with them and instructed them.

All this, however, was a prelude, a preparation for the New Covenant with a people who were both Jew and Gentile — bonded, not by the flesh, but by the spirit. The covenant is sealed in the Blood of Christ, who is the Head of the People of God.

The Spirit that anointed Him flows from Him to the Body — the people. One becomes a member of the People of God through faith in Jesus Christ and Baptism.

The Mission of the Church

Para. 782–786

What is the mission of the Catholic Church? According to the *Catechism*, the mission of the Church is to be "the salt of the earth and the light of the world." Its final destiny is the Kingdom of God begun by God Himself on earth, and will be perfected by Him at the end of time.

Jesus Christ is the one the Father anointed with the Holy Spirit to be Priest, Prophet, and King. The Church members share in these three offices and are responsible for continuing this mission.

Christ has made His new people a kingdom of priests to God. For the Christian to reign is to serve just as the King and Lord of the Universe made Himself servant of all. When we are serving someone poor and suffering, we recognize in him our poor and suffering Founder.

The Church Is the Body of Christ

Para. 787–789

What do we mean when we say the Church is the Body of Christ? From the very beginning, Jesus shared with His apostles His mission, His joys, His sufferings, and the mystery of the Kingdom. The *Catechism* points out that Jesus indicated the intimacy of His union with His followers when He said, "I am the vine, you are the branches. ... He who eats my flesh and drinks my blood abides in me, and I in him."

When Jesus' visible Presence was taken away from the apostles, they were not orphaned. Jesus sent them His Spirit. "As a result," says the *Catechism*, "communion with Jesus has become, in a way, more intense."

Jesus mystically constitutes as His body all those brethren called together from every nation. The Church is not only gathered around Christ — she is united in Him in His Body.

An Intimate Union

Believers who respond to God's Word and become members of Christ's Body become intimately united to Him, the *Catechism* tells us. Through the Sacraments, those who believe are actually joined with Christ in a very real and hidden way.

The Body's unity does not do away with the diversity of its members, who engage in a diversity of functions. The *Catechism* states, "The unity of the Mystical Body triumphs over all human divisions. ... 'There is neither Jew nor Greek, there is neither slave nor free, there is neither male nor female; for you are all one in Christ Jesus.'"

All are one in the Body of Christ. Christ is the Head of the body of the Church; the Principal of creation and redemption. We are united with Christ in His Passover. All His members must strive to resemble Him until Christ is formed in them.

Christ's Relationship to His Church

How does one describe Christ's relationship to His Church? The *Catechism* says Christ is one with His Church. He is the Head. We are the members. Head and members together make up the whole Body of Christ. Head and members form, as it were, one and the same mystical person.

Saint Joan of Arc put it very simply to her judges when she said, "About Jesus Christ and the Church, I simply know they're just one thing, and we shouldn't complicate the matter."

The *Catechism* also refers to the imagery of the bridegroom: the theme of Christ as the bridegroom of the Church as two within one relationship. Just as in marriage, "'two will become one flesh," and "the Church is the spotless bride of the spotless Lamb."

Christ has joined the Church with Himself in an everlasting covenant.

The Church as the Bride of Christ

What is Jesus Christ's relationship to the Church He founded? According to the *Catechism*, whether the head or the members of the Church speak, it is Christ who speaks in His role as the Head and in His role as the Body.

As Head, Christ calls Himself the "bridegroom." In the Gospel, Jesus says, "So they are no longer two, but one flesh." This great mystery of conjugal union, where two different persons become one, is applied to Christ and the Church.

The *Catechism* further says that the Church is the temple of the Holy Spirit. Saint Augustine said, "What the soul is to the human body, the Holy Spirit is to the Body of Christ, which is the Church." The Holy Spirit makes the Church "the temple of the living God."

The Work of the Holy Spirit
in the Church

Para. 797–801

What does the Holy Spirit do for the Church? The *Catechism* tells us that behind every vital and saving action in each part of the Body (the Church) is the Holy Spirit.

There are numerous venues through which the Holy Spirit works to build up the body in charity: through Baptism, through the Sacraments, through the grace of the apostles, through the virtues, and through charisms.

Charisms are special graces from the Holy Spirit that directly or indirectly benefit the Church. The *Catechism* describes a charism as a "wonderfully rich grace for the apostolic vitality and for the holiness of the entire Body of Christ, provided they really are genuine gifts of the Holy Spirit and are used in full conformity with authentic promptings of this same Spirit, that is, in keeping with charity, the true measure of all charisms."

Unity: The Essence of the Catholic Church

Para. 811–813

What is the essence of the Catholic Church? Unity, according to the *Catechism*.

In the Creed we profess the Catholic Church to be the sole Church of Christ, when we confess it to be one, holy, catholic, and apostolic. These are the essential features of the Church and her mission. Only faith can recognize these properties coming from her Divine Source.

Even historically, however, there are manifestations of this origin. "'Her marvelous propagation, eminent holiness, and inexhaustible fruitfulness in everything good, her catholic unity and invincible stability,'" the *Catechism* says, give evidence of credibility and irrefutable witness to her divine mission.

The Church is one because of her Divine Source. "'The highest exemplar and source of this mystery is the unity, in the Trinity of Persons, of one God, the Father and the Son in the Holy Spirit,'" the *Catechism* states.

Diversity in the Church

Para. 813–815

Does unity in the Church eliminate diversity? No, says the *Catechism*.

From the beginning, the Catholic Church has been marked by great diversity: diversity in God's gifts, and diversity in the multiplicity of cultures and people who are its members. There is even diversity in its "particular" churches that maintain their own traditions. The *Catechism* asserts this is not a threat to the Church's unity.

Sin, however, and its consequences are a constant threat to unity. The number-one bond of unity, the *Catechism* states, is charity, which "binds everything together in perfect harmony."

There are also visible bonds of unity: profession of one faith; common celebration of divine worship; and, especially, the Sacraments and apostolic succession through the Sacrament of Holy Orders.

Unity in Christ's Church

How important was unity to Jesus Christ? Very, according to the *Catechism*. He bestowed unity on His Church at the outset. It is something the Church can never lose — but with prayer and work, she can improve.

This is why, the *Catechism* says, Jesus Himself prayed at the hour of His Passion and continues praying, "That they may all be one. As you, Father, are in me and I am in you, may they also be one in us."

The *Catechism* further states, "The desire to recover the unity of all Christians is a gift of Christ and a call of the Holy Spirit." There are "certain things," the *Catechism* adds, required in order to respond adequately to this call: a permanent renewal of the Church, prayer in common, fraternal knowledge of each other, ecumenical formation, dialogue among theologians and Christians, and collaboration in good works.

Furthermore, there is conversion of the heart: "'try to live holier lives according to the Gospel'; for it is the unfaithfulness of the members to Christ's gift which causes divisions."

The Church Is Holy

Can a Church made up of sinners still be holy? Saint Thérèse, the "Little Flower," says this about the Catholic Church:

> If the Church was a body composed of differ-
> ent members, it could not lack the noblest of
> all; it *must* have a Heart, and a Heart burning
> with love. And I realized that this love alone
> was the true motive force which enabled the
> other members of the Church to act. If it
> ceased to function, the Apostles would forget
> to preach the gospel, the Martyrs would refuse
> to shed their blood. Love, in fact, is the voca-
> tion which includes all others; it is a universe of
> its own — comprising all time and space — it's
> eternal!

The *Catechism* tells us that our divine Lord, who knew nothing of sin, came only to expiate sin. Hence the Church gathers sinners already caught up in Christ's salvation, but still on the way to holiness.

The Church Is Sanctified by Christ

Why is the Church always considered holy? The Church is held to be holy because Jesus Christ — who alone with the Father and the Holy Spirit is holy — loved the Church as His bride. The *Catechism* tells us Jesus gave Himself up for her so as to sanctify her and endow her with the gift of the Holy Spirit for God's glory.

United with Christ, the Church is sanctified by Christ. With Him and through him, she becomes sanctifying. All the activities of the Church are directed toward the sanctification of persons in Christ and the glorification of God. It is in the Church that, by the grace of God, we acquire holiness.

The Church on earth already is endowed with real, though imperfect, sanctity. "In her members perfect holiness is something yet to be acquired," the *Catechism* states, though all members are called to perfect holiness. Charity is considered the soul of holiness.

The Church and Perfection

Where has the Church reached perfection? In the person of the Blessed Mother, according to the *Catechism*, "without spot or wrinkle." We the faithful are still striving to conquer sin and increase in holiness.

The word "catholic" means "universal." The Church is catholic in a double sense. First, the Church is catholic because Christ is present in her. "Where there is Christ Jesus, there is the Catholic Church," says the *Catechism*. From Him, she receives the fullness of the means of salvation: correct and complete confession of faith, full sacramental life, and ordained ministry in apostolic succession.

Second, the Church is catholic because she has been sent by Christ to the whole human race. In the beginning God made human nature one, and has decreed that all His children who were scattered should finally be gathered together as one.

Who Belongs to the Catholic Church?

Para. 836–838

Who belongs to the Catholic Church? According to the *Catechism*, all men and women are called to the "catholic unity of the people of God." In different ways they belong, or are ordered to belong.

The Catholic faithful, other believers in Christ, and all mankind are called by God's grace to salvation. Those who in faith accept all the precepts, Sacraments, and all the means of salvation given to the Church and possess the Spirit of Christ are fully incorporated into the society of the Church.

One who does not persevere in charity, however, is not saved. The *Catechism* states, "He remains indeed in the bosom of the Church, but 'in body,' not 'in heart.'"

The Church is joined in many ways to other faiths that call themselves Christian, even though they do not profess the Catholic faith in its entirety or have not preserved unity or communion under the successors of St. Peter. Those "who believe in Christ," the *Catechism* explains, "and have been properly baptized are put in a certain, although imperfect, communion with the Catholic Church."

The Catholic Church and Non-Christians

Para. 839–845

How are the People of God — the Church — related to religions who have yet to receive the Gospel? According to the *Catechism*, the Church is linked to the Jewish religion.

The Jews were the first to hear the Word of God. The Jewish faith is already a response to God's revelation in the Old Covenant. "To the Jews 'belong the sonship, the glory, the covenants, the giving of the law, the worship, and the promises,'" the *Catechism* asserts. "'To them belong the patriarchs, and of their race, according to the flesh, is the Christ'; 'for the gifts and the call of God are irrevocable.'"

The Muslims are related to the Church in that they acknowledge the Creator, profess to hold the faith of Abraham, and adore the one merciful God, mankind's judge on the last day.

The Church's bond with other non-Christian religions stems from the common belief in the origin and end of the human race, which in both cases is our Creator: God.

Why Do We Need Church?

Para. 845–848

Why do we have "Church"? The *Catechism* tells us that in order to reunite His children everywhere, God the Father willed to call everyone into His Son's Church.

The ark that Noah built prefigures the Church. Based on Scripture and Tradition, the *Catechism* says "that the Church, a pilgrim now on earth, is necessary for salvation."

Christ is the one mediator, the sole way of salvation. He is present to us in His Body, which is the Church. Jesus explicitly described the necessity of faith and Baptism for salvation, affirming the need for the Church. Those who know this and refuse to become part of the Church cannot be saved.

This statement excludes those who, through no fault of their own, know neither Christ nor the Church.

Mission — A Requirement
of Catholicity

Para. 849–851

When the Founder of the Catholic Church, Jesus
Christ, instructed His first "staff," the apostles, to
go forth and teach all nations, He gave them a mission. That mission is central to the lifeblood of the
Church: inviting people to share the communion of
the Father and the Son in the Spirit of Love.

The Church's missionary zeal and vigor come
from God's love for all mankind and His desire that
all be saved. The *Catechism* tells us that "God wills
the salvation of everyone through the knowledge of
the truth. Salvation is found in the truth."

The Spirit of truth prompts souls, and those
souls who respond are already on their way to salvation. But it is the obligation of the Church to reach
out to those desiring truth, so as to bring it to them.
"Because she believes in God's universal plan of salvation," the *Catechism* declares, "the Church must
be missionary."

Who Leads the Church?

Para. 849–855

Who leads the Church on its missionary path through history? The principal agent is the Holy Spirit, according to the *Catechism*.

Urged on by the Spirit of Christ, the Church must walk the path Christ trod, a way of poverty and obedience, service and self-sacrifice, even unto death. The "blood of martyrs is the seed of Christians," says the *Catechism*.

Throughout her history, the Church has experienced the discrepancy between the message and some of the messengers. That is why she follows the way of the Cross, a way of penance and renewal, to extend Christ's reign. The process of evangelizing involves bringing the Gospel to ears that have never before heard it — establishing God's presence through Christian communities and eventually local churches.

"There will be times of defeat," the *Catechism* admits, as the Church touches individuals and communities "'and so receives them into a fullness which is Catholic.'"

The Church Is Apostolic

How can the Catholic Church claim to be missionary and apostolic? The *Catechism* teaches that the Church's missionary task continues through worldwide evangelization and dialogue with non-believers. Believers can benefit from this dialogue through encounters with elements of truth and grace found in other religions and worldviews, which reflect the work of the secret presence of God in the hearts and minds of non-believers.

The *Catechism* asserts that the Church is apostolic because "she was and remains built on 'the foundation of the Apostles,' the witnesses chosen and sent on mission by Christ himself."

With the assistance of the Holy Spirit, the Church keeps and hands on the teaching of the apostles, and she continues to be taught, sanctified, and guided by the apostles through their successors, the College of Bishops, assisted by priests in union with the Pope until Jesus' return.

From Whence the Bishops?

Where did the Catholic Church get the office of bishop? From Jesus, who was the emissary of the Father. He said he did nothing except through the Father. As He was the Father's emissary, the apostles were His emissaries whom He specifically commissioned to carry on His mission.

As Jesus could do nothing without the Father, the apostles could do nothing without Him. He was the vine. They were the branches.

One aspect of the apostles' office could not be transmitted, and that was their witness to the Resurrection. Thus, they were the foundation stones of the Church.

Their office did, however, have a permanent aspect. The Divine Mission entrusted by Christ was designated by Him to continue to the end of time. The apostles, therefore, designated successors, and those successors designated their successors, down to this day. These are the bishops.

Apostolates
Para. 863–865

All of us, clergy and laity alike, have an apostolate, the *Catechism* teaches. An apostolate is defined in the *Catechism* as "'every activity of the Mystical Body' that aims 'to spread the Kingdom of Christ over all the earth.'"

The source of the Church's apostolate is Christ. So the fruitfulness of an apostolate depends on the apostle's union with Christ. Thus, charity, says the *Catechism*, "drawn from the Eucharist above all, is always, 'as it were, the soul of the whole apostolate.'"

The Kingdom of God has already come in the Person of Jesus Christ, and continues to grow in a mysterious way in the hearts of those incorporated in Him, until its full eschatological manifestation. "Then," the *Catechism* promises, "all those he has redeemed and made 'holy and blameless' ... will be gathered together as one People of God."

Who Are the Christian Faithful?

Para. 871–873

Just who are the Christian faithful? The Christian faithful are those who have been incorporated into Christ through Baptism and thus constitute the People of God. Since they have been reborn in Christ, they are equal in terms of dignity and activity in which they engage to build up the body of Christ according to their own circumstances.

The *Catechism* tells us there is "diversity of ministry but unity of mission," and the very differences that God has willed to put between the members of His Body actually serve this unity and mission.

The roles of teaching, sanctifying, and governing are the tasks given to the hierarchy. The laity are made "to share in the priestly, prophetical, and kingly office of Christ; they have therefore, in the Church and in the world, their own assignment in the mission of the whole People of God."

Hierarchical Constitution
of the Church

Para. 874–879

From where does the Catholic Church derive its ecclesial ministry? Jesus Christ is the source of all ministry in the Church, says the *Catechism*, and He set it up in "a variety of offices" that aim at the good of the whole body.

In a Letter to the Romans, St. Paul raised the question that illuminated the need for ministry. "How are they," he asked, "to believe in him of whom they have never heard? And how are they to hear without a preacher?" Paul pointed out, "Faith comes from what is heard."

No one can give himself the mandate and the mission to proclaim the Gospel. It comes by virtue of Christ's authority, through the Sacraments by which His ministers are given God's grace to do and give what they cannot do and give by their own powers.

Ecclesial ministry is also marked by the character of service. The ministers become "slaves of Christ," who became a slave Himself to save and redeem us.

The College of Bishops

Is the ecclesial ministry of the Catholic Church personal as well as sacramental and collegial in character? The *Catechism* says yes.

Jesus Christ, the founder of the Catholic Church, calls His ministers personally when He says, "Follow me." The College of Bishops is related to the pontiff in Rome, as Peter was related to the rest of the apostles.

When Christ instituted the twelve apostles, He constituted them in a college or permanent assembly, at the head of which He placed Peter, the "Rock" of His Church. Our Lord gave Peter the keys to His Church, designating him the shepherd of the whole flock. The power Christ gave Peter to loose and to bind was also given to the "college of apostles," but only united to its head, the pope.

"This pastoral office of Peter and the other apostles," the *Catechism* explains, "belongs to the Church's very foundation and is continued by the bishops under the primacy of the Pope."

Authority in the Catholic Church

How is authority structured in the Catholic Church? Christ is the source of all authority in the Church.

The Lord made St. Peter the "rock" of His Church — the shepherd of the whole flock. "The *Pope*, Bishop of Rome and Peter's successor, 'is the perpetual and visible source and foundation of the unity both of the bishops and the whole company of the faithful,'" according to the *Catechism*. Thus His successor, the pope and Vicar of Christ on earth, has "full, supreme and universal power ... which he can always exercise unhindered."

The College of Bishops has no power unless linked to the Roman pontiff. When united to the pope as its head, the College has supreme and full authority over the Universal Church. But that power cannot be exercised without the agreement of the Roman pontiff.

The College of Bishops exercises power over the Church in an ecumenical council, but, the *Catechism* reminds us, "there never is an ecumenical council which is not confirmed or at least recognized as such" by the pope.

Bishops: Heralds of Faith

Bishops in the Catholic Church are "heralds of faith," according to the *Catechism*. Their first task is to teach and preach the Gospel to all men and women.

In this, they are endowed with the authority of Christ. Christ, who is truth itself, willed to confer on the Church a share in His own infallibility in order that the people of God have true guidance as to Christ's teaching. Christ thus endowed the Church's shepherds with the gift of infallibility when instructing in matters of faith and morals.

The pope enjoys infallibility when he proclaims by a definitive act — a doctrine of faith and morals. This same infallibility is present in the College of Bishops only when, together with the pope, they exercise the supreme magisterium, particularly in an ecumenical council.

The Governing Office

The power the bishops exercise personally in the Name of Christ is "proper, ordinary, and immediate, although its exercise is ultimately controlled by the supreme authority of the Church," according to the *Catechism*.

The "Good Shepherd" should be the template of the bishop's pastoral office, and compassion for those who are ignorant and erring should be present as the bishop is aware of his own weaknesses. He should listen to his flock, the *Catechism* says.

The faithful should be closely attached to the bishop as the Church is close to Jesus Christ, and as Jesus Christ is to the Father.

Importance of the Lay Faithful

Para. 898–900

How important are the lay faithful to the life of the Catholic Church? Very important, according to the *Catechism*. When it comes to permeating the social, political, and economic realities with the demands of Christian doctrines and life, the initiative is particularly significant.

The *Catechism* quotes a discourse from Ven. Pope Pius XII: "Lay believers are in the front line of Church life; for them the Church is the animating principle of human society." They should have "an ever-clearer consciousness not only of belonging to the Church, but of being the Church. ... They have the right and duty, individually or grouped in associations, to work so that the divine message of salvation may be known and accepted by all men throughout the earth."

Their activity in ecclesial communities is so necessary, the *Catechism* continues, "that, for the most part, the apostolate of the pastors cannot be fully effective without it."

The Role of the Lay Faithful

Who is "king" in the eyes of the *Catechism*? The man who can govern his own body with "suitable rigor."

Jesus Christ, by His obedience unto death, conferred on man a "royal freedom." Through self-denial, men and women can "'overcome the reign of sin in themselves.'"

The *Catechism* further asserts that the laity, by uniting forces, can remedy spiritual malfunctions in institutions and conditions of the world. In so doing, "they will impregnate culture and human works with a moral value," according to *Lumen Gentium*, the Dogmatic Constitution on the Church from the Second Vatican Council.

Lay members of the Church can cooperate with their pastors in the service of the ecclesial community for the sake of its growth and life, by various ministries and by participating in councils, synods, and pastoral councils.

Consecrated Virgins

Para. 922–924

What is the history of consecrated virgins in the Church? From apostolic times, according to the *Catechism*, women have chosen to live as consecrated virgins, existing only for the Lord, clinging just to Him with greater freedom of heart, mind, body, and soul.

They are consecrated to God by the diocesan bishop according to the approved liturgical rite. They are betrothed, says the *Catechism*, "mystically to Christ." In the solemn rite they undergo, they become "a sacred person, a transcendent sign of the Church's love for Christ, and an eschatological image of this heavenly Bride of Christ and the life to come."

A consecrated virgin lives in the world, devoted to prayer, penance, and service to others. She engages in apostolic activity according to the state of life and spiritual gifts given to her. Consecrated virgins may form themselves into associations in order to live their commitment more faithfully.

The Communion of Saints

What is another name for the "Communion of Saints," a phrase frequently intoned by the Catholic Church?

The *Catechism* raises the question, "What is the Church if not the Assembly of all the saints?" Then it continues on to assert, "The communion of saints is the Church."

The faithful form one body. Therefore the good of one is communicated to all. The most important Member of the body is Jesus Christ, since He is the Head. He communicates His riches to all the other members through the Sacraments.

This is summed up in the Latin phrase "*Sancta, Sancti*," which means communion in holy things (*sancta*) among holy people (*sancti*).

The Communion of Sacraments

When we speak in the Catholic Church about the "Communion of the Sacraments," what do we mean?

According to the *Catechism*, "The fruit of all the sacraments belongs to all the faithful. All the sacraments are the sacred links uniting the faithful with one another and binding them to Jesus Christ, and above all Baptism, the gate by which we enter into the Church."

The name "communion" can be applied to all the Sacraments for they unite us to God, but most especially to the Eucharist, because "it is primarily the Eucharist that brings this communion about." In the "Communion of Charisms," the Holy Spirit distributes special and diverse graces among the "faithful of every rank" in order to build up the Church.

The phrase "They had everything in common" means that everything "the true Christian has is to be regarded as a good possessed in common with everyone else." Thus, a Christian should be eager to share whenever, wherever, with whomever has a need.

The Communion of the Church in Heaven and Earth

Para. 954–959

The *Catechism* has some very consoling words for those who have lost loved ones in death. It tells us that when Christ returns in glory, surrounded by His angels, everything and everyone will be subject to Him and death will be no more.

In the here and now, however, some disciples are pilgrims on earth; some are in the purification process; and some are in Heaven where God is visible to them as He really is. The *Catechism* teaches that souls in this state are still united to their loved ones on earth, and "this union is reinforced by an exchange of spiritual goods." Since these souls are "more closely united to Christ ... they do not cease to intercede with the Father."

The Many Communions

Para. 957–962

"Communion" is a very important word in the Catholic faith, referring to many things. The *Catechism* tells us that the "Communion of Saints" refers to the "holy things," foremost to the Eucharist by which the unity of believers — one body in Christ — is represented and brought about.

"Communion of Saints" also refers to "holy persons" in Christ who, the *Catechism* says, "'died for all' so that what each one does or suffers in and for Christ bears fruit for all." Then there is the Communion of the Faithful: the pilgrims on earth, those who are being purified for Heaven and those who are already in Heaven.

All together they form one Church. In this communion, we believe "the merciful love of God and his saints is always [attentive] to our prayers."

Mary's Assumption into Heaven

Para. 966–970

What does the *Catechism* teach us about the Assumption of the Virgin Mary? The Church professes that she was assumed into Heaven body and soul, honored by her Lord and Son as Queen of Heaven and all things.

By her Assumption, she participates in Christ's Resurrection and anticipates the resurrection of other Christians. She is a preeminent and wholly unique member of the Church as a result of her total obedience to the Father's will and her Son's redemptive work. Thus she is the Church's model of charity and faith.

According to the *Catechism*, Mary's motherhood "in the order of grace" continues in Heaven. What began with her assent to the Annunciation continued until she stood under the Cross, and will not cease until the eternal fulfillment of all the elect.

"The Blessed Virgin," the *Catechism* says, "is invoked in the Church under the titles of Advocate, Helper, Benefactress, and Mediatrix."

Mary's Role
Para. 970–971

What does the *Catechism* teach us about the Church's devotion to the Virgin Mary? "The Church's devotion to the Blessed Virgin," the *Catechism* tells us, "is intrinsic to Christian worship."

"From the most ancient times the Blessed Virgin has been honored with the title of 'Mother of God,' to whose protection the faithful fly in all dangers and needs."

Liturgical feasts dedicated to Mary along with Marian prayer such as the Rosary express this devotion.

Mary's function as mother of men in no way obscures or diminishes the unique mediation of Christ, the *Catechism* states. In fact, Mary's role derives its power from her Son's role. Just as the priesthood of Christ is shared in many ways both by His priests and the faithful, so is His mediation shared with the Blessed Mother.

The Forgiveness of Sins

When the Risen Christ conferred the ability to forgive sins on the apostles and their successors, He gave them participation in His own divine power.

Jesus tied forgiveness of sins to faith and Baptism when He instructed the apostles, "Go onto all the world and preach the gospel to the whole creation. He who believes and is baptized will be saved."

In making the first profession of faith while receiving Baptism, the new Christian has not only original sin cleansed from his soul but all sins committed through his own will and all punishment due to sin. Baptism does not, however, erase the weakness of human nature. We are still subject to the wiles of concupiscence, which never ceases to lead us toward evil.

Thus the Church's power to forgive sins extends beyond Baptism to the Sacrament of Penance.

The Resurrection of the Body

Para. 997–1001

What is the most opposed belief of the Christian faith? The *Catechism* tells us it is our belief that our body will rise again after death.

That there is some kind of spiritual existence after death is a fairly common belief. It is the resurrection of the mortal body that challenges the imagination. How can this happen?

We rise again through the power of Christ's Resurrection. Just as He was raised with His own Body, so shall we be raised. The *Catechism* states, "Christ 'will change our lowly body to be like his glorious body,' into a 'spiritual body.'"

Our earthly body, which decays after death, will be rejoined to the soul and will never again be subject to decay.

Risen with Christ

Do we have assurance that we will rise with Christ in the last days?

In his First Letter to the Corinthians, St. Paul writes, "The body is meant for the Lord and the Lord for the body." God, who raised up Christ, will also raise us up on the last day.

The *Catechism* tells us, "To rise with Christ, we must die with Christ: we must 'be away from the body and at home with the Lord.'" Death is the separation of the body from the soul. "For those who die in Christ's grace," the *Catechism* states, "it is a participation in the death of the Lord, so that we can share his Resurrection."

The normality of death leads to a sense of urgency in our lives, helping us to realize that we have only a limited amount of time to bring our lives to fulfillment.

Fear of Death

Para. 1010–1014

Why do we fear death? Death seems to hold such terror for modern man that we seldom use the word "die." Our loved ones do not die. They "pass away." Some folk even shorten the distance to a mere "pass."

Pass where? Pass what? Is this a form of denial?

The *Catechism* tells us that death should not be a fearful event for the practicing Christian, as it is the moment God calls the soul to Himself. Saint Paul actually yearned for death. "My desire," he said, "is to depart and be with Christ."

Saint Teresa of Ávila agreed. "I want to see God," she declared. "In order to see him, I must die." The Little Flower proclaimed, "I am not dying. I am entering eternal life."

The *Catechism* advises us to be prepared for the hour of our death. "Why not keep clear of sin instead of running away from death?" St. Thomas à Kempis wrote in *The Imitation of Christ*. "If you aren't fit for death today, it's very unlikely you will be tomorrow."

In short, live every moment as though it were your last.

What is Heaven?

What is Heaven? Where is it? How do we get there? Almost from the moment we arrive on earth, we wonder where we're going when we leave it.

According to the *Catechism*, Heaven is "this perfect life with the Most Holy Trinity — this communion of life and love with the Trinity, with the Virgin Mary, the angels, and all the blessed. ... Heaven is the ultimate end and fulfillment of the deepest human longings, the state of supreme, definitive happiness."

Being in Heaven is to be with Christ. The elect, the *Catechism* states, "live 'in Christ,'" yet they retain their own name, finding their true identity.

How do we get to Heaven? The *Catechism* lays out the route. We are baptized in the faith and then we must live it, so that we die in God's grace and friendship.

Amen, Its Root and Meaning

What is the root and the multiple meanings of a word we say so often: "Amen"?

As described in the *Catechism,* in Hebrew, Amen's root is the same as the word "believe." It expresses solidity, trustworthiness, and faithfulness. Thus, in our prayers, "Amen" may express both God's faithfulness to us and our trust in Him.

The Lord Jesus frequently used the word "Amen," sometimes twice in one sentence, to emphasize the trustworthiness of His teaching and His authority founded on God's truth. He himself is the definitive Amen of the Father's love for us.

"For all the promises of God find their Yes in him," says the *Catechism*, which "is why we utter the Amen through him, to the glory of God."

PART TWO:

THE CELEBRATION OF THE CHRISTIAN MYSTERY

Christian/Jewish Similarities

Are there similarities between Christian and Jewish liturgies? There are indeed, according to the *Cate-chism*, which states, "A better knowledge of the Jewish people's faith and religious life ... can help our better understanding of certain aspects of Christian liturgy."

Sacred Scripture is an essential part of both liturgies, such as proclamation of the Word of God, the response to it, and the intercessions for the living and the dead. The Liturgy of the Hours, the Lord's Prayer, as well as other venerable prayers and texts have parallels in Jewish prayer. Christian Eucharistic prayers also draw their inspiration from the Jewish tradition.

During the Easter season, the similarities and the differences of the two religions are most evident. The Jews celebrate Passover as history tending toward a future event. Christians view the Passion and death of Christ as fulfilling the Passover, while still anticipating its definitive consummation.

Celebrants of the Heavenly Liturgy

In the Book of Revelation, St. John speaks of seeing the mighty visions with symbols the Church needs to, and does, interpret for the reader. John writes of a "throne … in heaven, with one seated on the throne: the Lord God." Then he speaks of a lamb, as though slain, standing to the right. This is Jesus, crucified and risen.

Finally, the passage points to a "river of the water of life … flowing from the throne of God and of the Lamb." This is a symbol of the Holy Spirit. The "four living beings" signify all creation. The 24 elders are the servants of the Old and New Covenants. The 144,000 are the new people of God. The "woman" is the Blessed Mother.

"It is in this eternal liturgy," the *Catechism* states, "that the Spirit and the Church enable us to participate whenever we celebrate the mystery of salvation in the sacraments."

What Time's the Liturgy?

When are the most important times to celebrate the Liturgy? According to the *Catechism*, Holy Mother Church has decreed that there are certain days throughout the year when the saving work of Christ should be commemorated.

The Lord's Resurrection is celebrated once a week on Sunday, the Lord's Day. Once a year, it is also celebrated along with His Passion at Easter. Easter is considered by the Church to be the most solemn of all feasts.

During the course of the year, the Church's liturgy unfolds the "whole mystery of Christ," and it is made present to the faithful in every age. "When the Church celebrates the mystery of Christ," says the *Catechism*, "there is a word that marks her prayer: 'Today!' — a word echoing the prayer her Lord taught her and the call of the Holy Spirit."

This "today" in God's time always makes present the hour of Jesus' Passover, "which reaches across and underlies all history." Saint Hippolytus described this as "a day of long, eternal light ... ushered in for us who believe in him, a day which is never blotted out: the mystical Passover."

Baptism:
Gateway to Life in the Spirit
Para. 1213–1216

Why is Baptism so crucial to salvation? According to the *Catechism*, "Baptism is the basis of the whole Christian life, the gateway to life in the Spirit, and the door which gives access to all the other sacraments."

The term "baptism" comes from the Greek word *bapizein*, which means "to immerse." The immersion or plunge into water during the Sacrament symbolizes the catechumen's burial into Christ's death, from which He rises up with Christ as "a new creature."

Another name for the Sacrament is the "washing of regeneration and renewal by the Holy Spirit," because it signifies the birth of water and the Spirit, without which we cannot enter into the Kingdom of God.

Everything Points to Jesus

Everything points to Jesus. "All the Old Covenant prefigurations find their fulfillment in Christ Jesus," according to the *Catechism.*

The Lord began His public ministry after He voluntarily submitted Himself to Baptism as performed by John the Baptist. The immersion in the Jordan was intended for sinners, but for Jesus it was to fulfill all righteousness, says the Gospel of Matthew. It was a manifestation of Jesus' self-emptying.

The Spirit, who had hovered over the waters of the first creation, descended on Jesus as a prelude to the New Creation. The Father revealed Jesus as His "beloved Son."

In His Passion, the *Catechism* tells us, Jesus opened to all the fountain of Baptism. The blood and water that flowed from the side of Christ are "types of Baptism and the Eucharist, the sacraments of new life."

Who May Be Baptized?

Who may be baptized into the Catholic faith? The *Catechism* tells us that Baptism may only be administered to a person who has never been previously baptized.

When an adult is baptized, he undergoes a preparation for the Sacrament called the Catechumenate. The candidate for Baptism is called a Catechumen. The Catechumen should be properly initiated into the mystery of salvation and the practice of the evangelical virtues. They should also be introduced into the life of faith, liturgy, and charity of the People of God by successive rites.

Baptism of infants is, the *Catechism* says, "an immemorial tradition of the Church." Church law urges that a child be baptized as soon after birth as possible, in order that the baby not be denied the priceless grace of becoming a child of God.

The Origin of Confirmation

Para. 1285–1288

What does the *Catechism* tell us about prophecies in the Old Testament concerning a Messiah? The Old Testament, according to the *Catechism*, foretold the coming of a Messiah on whom the Spirit of the Lord would rest.

When God spoke after John the Baptist baptized Jesus in the Jordan River, this was the sign that the Messiah had arrived and that Jesus was He. The fullness of the Spirit was not only to rest on the Messiah, but was to be communicated to the whole messianic people.

Jesus, on several occasions, promised this outpouring of the Spirit, and the promise was fulfilled on Easter Sunday and more visibly on Pentecost.

The laying on of hands, the *Catechism* states, "is rightly recognized by the Catholic tradition as the origin of the sacrament of Confirmation, which in a certain way perpetuates the grace of Pentecost in the Church."

Anointing with Hands and Oil

Para. 1286–1289

From the time of the first Pentecost, in order to fulfill Christ's will, the apostles administered the laying on of hands to the newly baptized. This imparts the Spirit, which completes the grace of Baptism.

The imposition of hands is recognized as the origin of Confirmation. Very early in the Church, anointing with oil called chrism was added to the laying on of hands.

In the Eastern Church, the Sacrament is called chrismation. The name "Christian" means "anointed," calling to mind Jesus Whom the Father anointed with the Holy Spirit at His Baptism in the Jordan.

Confirmation:
Eastern and Western Traditions

Para. 1290–1292

When should you receive the Sacrament of Confirmation? In the first centuries, the *Catechism* tells us, Baptism and Confirmation were generally conferred together in what some referred to as a "double sacrament."

Confirmation is ordinarily conferred by the bishop in his role as apostolic successor. As time went on, the number of rural parishes and dioceses grew and infant baptisms multiplied, such that it became difficult for bishops to officiate. In the West, the desire to have the bishop administer Confirmation, which perfects baptismal grace, caused the temporal separation of the two Sacraments.

The Eastern tradition, however, has kept Baptism and Confirmation united, so that the priest administers both — Confirmation only being done with the "*myron*" or holy oil, which must be consecrated by a bishop.

The Effects of Confirmation

Para. 1293–1296

What happens to us when we receive Confirmation? What are the effects of the Sacrament?

The *Catechism* tells us that when Christians are confirmed, their baptismal grace is increased and deepened. They share more completely in the mission of the Lord Jesus. They are filled with the Holy Spirit, "so that their lives may give off 'the aroma of Christ.'"

The anointing of Confirmation, the *Catechism* further tells us, places on the confirmand the seal of the Holy Spirit, signifying "our total belonging to Christ, our enrollment in his service for ever, as well as the promise of divine protection in the great eschatological trial."

Significance of Anointing
in Confirmation

Para. 1293–1294

What is the significance of the anointing oil or chrism during the administration of Confirmation? According to the *Catechism*, when a Christian is thus anointed, he is marked with a permanent spiritual seal. Anointing in biblical times was rich with symbolism.

"Oil is a sign of abundance and joy," the *Catechism* states. It cleanses and limbers the body. It is a sign of healing. Think of it being administered to cuts and bruises. It gives radiant beauty and strength. All these features of oil are present in the sacramental life.

"The pre-baptismal anointing with the oil of catechumens signifies cleansing and strengthening," says the *Catechism*. "Anointing of the sick expresses healing and comfort."

In Confirmation and Holy Orders, the post-baptismal anointing with sacred chrism denotes consecration.

Format of the Eucharistic Celebration

Para. 1345

The format of the Eucharistic celebration in the Catholic Church has remained virtually the same for almost 2,000 years.

Around AD 155, St. Justin Martyr explained the Mass to the pagan emperor, Antonius Pius. On the "day of the sun," he told Pius, Christians gather in the same place. "The memoirs of the apostles and the writings of the prophets are read." When the readings are finished, the presider "admonishes and challenges" those gathered "to imitate these beautiful things" just read.

The homily is followed by prayers of petition for those gathered and for all others. The "kiss" is exchanged. Then the presider is presented with offerings of water and wine and the bread, over which he prays extensively.

When the prayers are concluded, the deacons give to those present the consecrated bread and wine.

The Meaning of Eucharist

What is the significance of the Eucharist? The *Cat-echism* tells us that, in the Eucharist, we thank God our Father for all the benefits He has bestowed on us.

The Eucharist is "the sacrifice of praise by which the Church sings the glory of God in the name of all creation." The Eucharist is a memorial of Christ's Passion, death, and Resurrection. It does more than merely commemorate these events: it re-presents them, making them present and real.

Because it is a memorial of Christ's Passover, it is also a sacrifice. Christ gives us the very Body and Blood He gave up for us on the Cross.

Finally, the Eucharist is the Real Presence of Christ by the power of His Word and the Holy Spirit.

The Real Presence of Christ in the Eucharist

Para. 1373–1375

What is one of the most challenging doctrines of the Catholic Church to comprehend? It is the mystery of the Real Presence of Jesus Christ in the Sacrament of the Eucharist.

The *Catechism* tells us that Christ is present to His Church in many ways, but most especially in the Eucharistic species, and that His presence in these species of bread and wine is unique. "The whole Christ" — Body, Blood, Soul, and Divinity — "is truly, really, and substantially contained" therein. In other words, under sacramental signs, He is physically as well as spiritually present.

Saint John Chrysostom declares that man does not cause this miraculous occurrence: "The priest, in the role of Christ, pronounces these words, but their power and grace are God's."

It is Christ Himself who brings about the transformation of the bread and wine into His Body and Blood.

The Eucharist, the Sacrament of Love

Why would Jesus choose to be present under the humble circumstances of bread and wine? "It is highly fitting," says the *Catechism*, "that Christ should have wanted to remain present with his Church in this unique way."

In His Eucharistic Presence, Jesus is always within His Church in a sacramental and mysterious manner. Saint Cyril of Alexandria counseled, "Do not doubt whether this is true, but rather receive the words of the Savior in faith, for he is the truth, he cannot lie."

Pope St. John Paul II wrote, "The Church and the world have a great need for Eucharistic worship. Jesus awaits us in this sacrament of love."

The Pope urged we the faithful not to refuse the Lord the time to meet with Him, adoring him in contemplation, open to making amends for the serious crimes and offenses of the world.

The Paschal Banquet

The *Catechism* opens up the mystery and the true magnificence of the Mass. It is both the sacrificial memorial that perpetuates the sacrifice of the Cross and the sacred banquet of communion with Our Lord's Body and Blood.

The whole movement of the Eucharistic sacrifice is toward the faithful achieving union with Christ through reception of Holy Communion. The altar is both the altar of sacrifice and the table of the Lord. The Christian altar is a symbol of Christ. It represents, says St. Ambrose, "the body of Christ and the body of Christ is on the Altar."

Our Lord made it very clear how important it was for us to receive Him in the Eucharist. In John 6:53, He says, "Truly, I say to you, unless you eat the flesh of the Son of Man and drink his blood, you have no life within you."

Reception of the Holy Eucharist

Para. 1384–1389

How often does the Church require us to receive Our Blessed Lord in the Eucharist?

A Catholic is required to receive Holy Communion at least once a year — if possible, during the Easter season. The Second Vatican Council, however, warmly recommended that properly prepared faithful receive Communion every time they participate in Mass.

We are obliged to attend the Divine Liturgy on Sundays and Holy Days, but we are encouraged to participate more often, even daily.

The *Catechism* also cautions, however, against a sacrilegious reception of the Sacrament, quoting St. Paul's stern admonition: "Whoever, therefore, eats the bread or drinks the cup of the Lord in an unworthy manner will be guilty of profaning the body and blood of the Lord," bringing judgment upon himself.

How Should We Receive the King?

Para. 1384–1391

What is the purpose of receiving the Holy Eucharist? The *Catechism* tells us that the principal reason is an intimate union with Jesus Christ, who is sacramentally and really present in the bread and the wine. Even if we receive just one of the species, we fully receive Christ.

There are requirements and proper dispositions for receiving so great a Sacrament. Our souls must be free of mortal sin. We are required to fast from food and drink for one hour before Communion.

We should wear appropriate clothing and assume the proper reverent gesture in order to reflect the proper solemnity, joy, and respect when Christ becomes our guest.

A Pledge of the Glory to Come

The Holy Eucharist is fulfillment for the present day and a taste of heavenly glory. The *Catechism* quotes an ancient prayer of the Church, which says, in part, "O sacred banquet in which Christ is received as food, the memory of the Passion is renewed, the soul is filled with grace and a pledge of the life to come is given to us."

Jesus pointed this fact out to His apostles at the Last Supper, indicating the fulfillment of His Passion, death, and Resurrection in the Kingdom of God: "I tell you, I shall not drink again of the fruit of the vine until that day when I drink it new with you in my Father's kingdom."

Though we know Christ's Real Presence is in our midst now, that Presence is veiled. So we wait and pray for the day when our Savior comes again, and we will see our God as He is.

Healing Both Body and Soul

Think of Our Lord Jesus Christ as the physician of both our bodies and souls. Through His Church, He has willed that the same healing power that forgave the paralytic his sins and empowered him to pick up his mat and walk be transmitted to members of the Church today. This takes place through the two Sacraments of Healing: Penance and the Anointing of the Sick.

The *Catechism* tells us that those who go to Confession obtain God's mercy for their sins and are reconciled to God and to the Church, which they have wounded with their offenses.

Penance is called the "sacrament of conversion" because, in a sacramental venue, it makes present Jesus' call to conversion. It is called "confession" because relating our offenses to a priest is an essential part of the Sacrament.

The Need for Reconciliation

Why do we need the Sacrament of Reconciliation? After all, Baptism sanctified us, washed us, and justified us in the Name of the Lord Jesus and in the Spirit of God. What more do we need?

The *Catechism* reminds us that, for all Baptism does for us, "the new life received in Christian initiation has not abolished the frailty and weakness of human nature, nor the inclination to sin that tradition calls *concupiscence*." So we are engaged in a lifelong struggle of conversion that directs us toward holiness and eternal life.

It is a struggle that we will always need the aid of Christ's grace that comes to us, among other venues, through the Sacrament of Reconciliation and Penance.

Conversion
Para. 1430–1439

Conversion is talked about in 33 different sections of the *Catechism*. In one section, the *Catechism* describes conversion as "interior repentance," a radical realignment of one's life.

Conversion is a turning to God with a desire to leave sin and rely on God's mercy, trusting in the help of His grace. It is God's grace working within us that gives us a new heart, rendering us the strength to begin anew. Discovering God's great love for us drives us to the full realization of the weight of our sin and the wish to never offend Him again.

Conversion is not a one-time event; it has to be ongoing — a continual turning more and more toward God.

The chief forms of penance, as insisted upon by the Church Fathers and Scripture, are prayer, fasting, and almsgiving. There are also other means of attaining forgiveness of sin, such as an effort to reconcile with one's neighbor and concern for our neighbor's salvation.

Water and Tears of Conversion

What is conversion? The *Catechism* says there are two kinds of conversion: the first is Baptism, which removes original sin and washes away all other sin. The second is the conversion of the heart from sin to the merciful love of God. It is Jesus who calls us to this conversion.

"The time is fulfilled," Jesus said. "The kingdom of God is at hand; repent and believe in the Gospel." A perfect example of this conversion is St. Peter, who, after denying his Master three times, burst into tears of repentance.

Saint Ambrose describes the two conversions as "water and tears: the water of Baptism and the tears of repentance."

Jesus' call to conversion is not first and foremost to outward penances such as sackcloth and ashes, but to an interior conversion of the heart, without which penances are sterile and futile.

Eucharist and Penance

Para. 1434–1439

What does the Eucharist do for daily conversion and penance? The *Catechism* tells us we are fed by the Eucharist, for in it, Christ's sacrifice on the Cross — which reconciles us to God — is made present.

The Council of Trent declared that the Eucharist "is a remedy to free us from our daily faults and to preserve us from mortal sins." Such devotions as reading Sacred Scripture, praying the Liturgy of the Hours and the Our Father, and every sincere act of worship revives the spirit of conversion and repentance within us and contributes to the forgiveness of sins.

The *Catechism* cites the parable of the Prodigal Son with the very merciful father as a classic tale of conversion, saying only the Heart of Christ who knows the depth of His Father's love could reveal it to us in such a simple and beautiful way.

Who Forgives Our Sins?

Para. 1441–1445

When we receive the Sacrament of Reconciliation and hear that our sins are forgiven, do we realize that it is actually God forgiving our sins?

"Only God forgives sins," the *Catechism* asserts. But as the Son of God, Jesus shared His divine authority with His apostles, and gave them the power to forgive sins.

"Christ has willed that in her prayer and life and action his whole Church should be the sign and instrument of the forgiveness and reconciliation," says the *Catechism*. Jesus not only forgave sins, He integrated the sinner into the company of the people of God.

"A remarkable sign of this," states the *Catechism*, "is the fact that Jesus receives sinners at his table, a gesture that expresses in an astonishing way both God's forgiveness and the return to the bosom of the People of God."

The power to forgive sins was expressed in the power that Jesus bestowed on Simon Peter, when He gave Peter the keys to the Kingdom of Heaven.

The Why and How of Confession

Para. 1446–1447

Why do we have Confession? According to the *Catechism*, "Christ instituted the sacrament of Penance for all sinful members of his Church: above all for those who, since Baptism, have fallen into grave sin, and have thus lost their baptismal grace and wounded ecclesial communion."

Over the centuries, the administration of the Sacrament has evolved. In the early Church, penitents guilty of particularly grave offenses such as idolatry, adultery, and murder were required to do public penance — sometimes for years — before receiving reconciliation.

In the seventh century, Irish missionaries, inspired by Eastern monastic tradition, brought the practice of private penance to Europe. This effectively ended public penance before forgiveness, making the Sacrament essentially between penitent and priest as it is today.

Confession Frees

Para. 1455–1456

How can we think of Confession as liberation rather than intrusion? Confession "frees us and facilitates our reconciliation with others," the *Catechism* instructs us.

Through confession, we take a deep and honest look at ourselves and our sins and we take responsibility for them, thereby opening ourselves again to God and to the communion of the Church as well as a new future.

"Confession to a priest is an essential part of the sacrament," the *Catechism* states. All mortal sins of which the penitent is aware must be confessed, "even if they are most secret and have been committed against the last two precepts of the Decalogue [the Ten Commandments]; for these sins sometimes wound the soul more grievously and are more dangerous than [sins] committed openly."

Confessing Our Sins

Para. 1456–1458

What sins should Catholics mention in Confession? According to the *Catechism*, we are obliged to confess serious sin at least once a year.

Children must receive the Sacrament of Penance before receiving Holy Communion for the first time. Thereafter, a mortal sin must be confessed and sacramental absolution received before taking Communion unless there is a very grave reason for receiving Communion and there is no possibility of going to Confession.

Confessing all the sins a penitent can remember undoubtedly places him or her before the Divine Mercy for pardon. If, however, a penitent knowingly withholds sins, he places nothing before the Divine Goodness for remission through the priest.

Confessing venial sins is not strictly necessary, but is strongly urged by the Church in order to fight evil tendencies, strengthen our conscience, and let ourselves be healed by Christ.

Penance for Sins

How do we make satisfaction — do penance — for our sins? Absolution from a priest takes away sin, the *Catechism* tells us, but it does not remedy all the disorders that sin causes.

For instance, if we wrong our neighbors, we must repair the harm as far as possible (i.e., we must return stolen goods, restore the reputation of anyone we have slandered, or compensate the person we have injured).

Not only does sin hurt the person we have wounded, it injures the sinner. In order to regain our spiritual health, we must do something to make amends. That is where expiation for sin comes in. Thus, the priest confessor administers a penance for the person's spiritual good that is commensurate with the gravity of his or her sins.

Confession brings reconciliation not only with God but also with the Church.

Frequency of Confession

Para. 1461–1464

How often should one go to Confession? The *Catechism* tells us that priests are to encourage the faithful to come to the Sacrament of Penance and must make themselves available to celebrate the Sacrament whenever Christians reasonably ask for it.

Certain sins are so grave that they incur excommunication, the most severe Church penalty, "which impedes the reception of the sacraments and the exercise of certain ecclesiastical acts, and for which absolution consequently cannot be granted, according to canon law, except by the Pope, the bishop of the place or priests authorized by them."

If the penitent is in danger of death, any priest, even if deprived of faculties for the Rite of Confession, can absolve the penitent from every sin and excommunication.

Secrecy of the Sacrament of Penance

Can a priest ever reveal what he has heard in Confession? No, he cannot, the *Catechism* firmly states.

Due to the delicacy and greatness of this ministry and the respect due to persons, the Church declares that the priest must keep all he hears under the seal of the Sacrament. Under no circumstances may he disclose what he has heard in Confession. Were he to do so, he would face severe Church penalties.

When he is celebrating the Sacrament of Penance, the priest is fulfilling the ministry of the Good Shepherd seeking the lost sheep; the good Samaritan who binds up the wounds; the merciful Father who welcomes home the Prodigal Son; and the impartial judge whose judgment is just and merciful.

The confessor is the servant, not the master, of God's forgiveness, leading the penitent to maturity and healing.

Our Extended Family in Heaven

Who and what make up the "Communion of Saints"? According to the *Catechism*, the Communion of Saints, which forms one Church, is composed of the faithful in Heaven, the faithful expiating their sins in Purgatory, and those still walking their earthly journey.

The *Catechism* says there is a "perennial link of charity" that exists between the three groups. The holiness of one profits others much more than the sins of one can cause harm to others.

The spiritual goods of the Communion of Saints is called the Treasury of the Church. It is made up of the infinite value of the merits of Christ the Redeemer, which can never be exhausted before the Father: the prayers, the immense and unfathomable good works of the Blessed Mother, and the prayers and good works of all the saints.

The Anointing of the Sick

Para. 1499–1501

What takes place during the Sacrament that is called the Anointing of the Sick? According to the *Catechism*, when those who are ill are anointed with sacred oils, the Church commends them "to the suffering and glorified Lord, that he may raise them up and save them." The Church exhorts the sick person to unite their suffering to the Passion and death of Christ.

The *Catechism* acknowledges that illness and suffering are among the most difficult and serious problems that human beings confront. The patient faces his vulnerability, powerlessness, and perhaps a glimpse of death. Illness can lead to anger, self-absorption, and even revolt against God. On the other hand, it can and often does lead to a new maturity and a return to God.

The Divine Physician

Para. 1503–1506

Who is more important in our lives than our doctor? One of the tenderest ways to reflect on Jesus is as Christ the Divine Physician, the Healer of both body and soul.

During His earthly journey, Jesus showed great compassion for the sick and the suffering. The *Catechism* reminds us that the Lord healed every kind of infirmity, mental and physical, "a resplendent sign that 'God has visited his people.'" Yet the Lord did not cure everyone. His healings were meant to point to a more radical healing when He would — from the Cross — effect victory over sin and death.

Jesus invites His disciples to follow Him by taking up their cross in turn. By following Jesus, His disciples acquire a new outlook on the sick and suffering. They share in Jesus' ministry of compassion and healing.

Sacrament of the Sick

Para. 1510–1520

Which of the seven Sacraments has been especially instituted by Christ to aid those who are being tried by serious illness? It is the Sacrament called the Anointing of the Sick.

This Sacrament was particularly promulgated by the Apostle James, who said, "Is anyone among you sick? They should call for the elders of the church and have them pray over them, anointing them with oil in the name of the Lord. The prayer of faith will save the sick, and the Lord will raise them up; and anyone who has committed sins will be forgiven" (Jas 5:14-15).

Over the centuries, the Sacrament came to be used on those who were dying and was called Extreme Unction, but in this day and age it is seen not as a Sacrament strictly for those who are near death but also those who are gravely ill in the hope they will recover.

When Does Anointing Take Place?

Para. 1514–1515

When is it appropriate to request the Anointing of the Sick? The *Catechism* enlightens us to some beautiful truths concerning this Sacrament.

It is often thought to be given only at the point of death, but this is not true. As soon as one of the faithful begins to be in danger of death from sickness or old age, it is already time for them to receive the Sacrament. Should the sick person recover his or her health and then later become gravely ill once more, they may be anointed again.

If, during the same illness, the condition becomes more serious, they may receive the Sacrament yet another time. A patient may also be anointed prior to serious surgery, as well as when one grows quite frail during the elder years.

Graces Bestowed in Anointing of the Sick

Para. 1520–1522

Many graces are bestowed by the Holy Spirit during the Sacrament of the Sick, according to the *Catechism*, many of which we may not be aware.

The first grace is one of strengthening, peace, and courage to the patient in order that he or she may overcome the difficulties of serious illness or the frailty of old age. It helps to guard the sick person against the temptations of the devil to discouragement and anguish in the face of death. The grace is meant to lead to a healing of soul and the body as well, if the latter be the will of God. The sick person's sins will be forgiven if he or she is not able to obtain forgiveness through the Sacrament of Penance.

"The sick who receive this sacrament," the *Catechism* says, "by freely uniting themselves to the passion and death of Christ, contribute to the good of the People of God," for his or her own good, and for that of the whole Church.

Sacrament of the Dying

Para. 1523–1525

The Sacrament of the Sick is also called *sacramentum exeuntium* — the Sacrament of Those Departing, a preparation for the final journey.

The Anointing of the Sick, says the *Catechism*, "completes our conformity to the death and Resurrection of Christ, just as Baptism began it. It completes the holy anointings that mark the whole Christian life." Baptism seals the new life within us. Confirmation strengthens us for the combat of life. And the final anointing fortifies us for the last struggle before entering the Father's house.

The Church also offers the departing Catholic the Eucharist as Viaticum. Receiving Communion at this time of our life has particular significance, because it is the seed of eternal life and the power of the Resurrection. "The sacrament of Christ once dead and now risen, the Eucharist is here the sacrament of passing over from death to life, from this world to the Father," the *Catechism* states.

Holy Orders

What exactly is Holy Orders? According to the *Catechism*, it is the Sacrament "through which the mission entrusted by Christ to his apostles continues to be exercised in the Church until the end of time." It is thus the Sacrament of apostolic ministry. It includes three degrees: the episcopate (bishops), the presbyterate (priests), and the diaconate (deacons).

In the Old Covenant, God's chosen people were constituted by Him as "a kingdom of priests and a holy nation." But within the Israelites, God chose the tribe of Levi for liturgical service. "God himself is its inheritance," the *Catechism* states. "The priests are 'appointed to act on behalf of men in relation to God, to offer gifts and sacrifices for sins.'"

This Old Testament priesthood, however, was powerless to bring about definitive sanctification, which could only be achieved by the sacrifice of Christ.

Definition of Orders in Holy Orders

Para. 1537–1538

Where do we get the term "orders" when we talk about the Sacrament of Holy Orders?

In Roman antiquity, according to the *Catechism*, the term "orders" indicated an established civil body, especially a governing body. There are certain established bodies in the Church, and they are called *taxeis* or *ordines*.

Today the term "ordination" is reserved for men who become part of the order of bishops, presbyters (priests), and deacons. It goes beyond a simple election, designation, or institution by the community, for, the *Catechism* says, it "confers a gift of the Holy Spirit that permits the exercise of a 'sacred power' ... which can come only from Christ himself through his Church."

One True Priest

There is essentially one true Priest, says the *Catechism*, and that is Jesus Christ. All others are His ministers.

There is the common priesthood in which all of the baptized and confirmed faithful participate, according to their vocation. Bishops and priests make up the ministerial priesthood, which is essentially at the service of the common priesthood of the faithful.

Jesus is the one, unique Mediator between God the Father and the faithful. With a single offering, He brought about salvation, once and for all. Still, that sacrifice is made present through the celebration of the Mass.

The one priesthood of Christ "is made present through the ministerial priesthood without diminishing the uniqueness of Christ's priesthood," says the *Catechism*.

Source of All Priesthood

Who is the source of all priesthood? Jesus Christ, the *Catechism* tells us. The priest of the Old Law was a figure of Christ, and the priest of the New Law acts in the Person of Christ.

In the Mass, it is Christ Himself who is present to His Church as Head of His Body, Shepherd of His flock, High Priest of the Redemptive Sacrifice, and Teacher of Truth, says the *Catechism*.

By virtue of the Sacrament of Holy Orders, the priest acts *in persona Christi Capitis*. Christ is made visible in the community of believers through the ordained ministry. The bishop, in the words of St. Ignatius of Antioch, is like the living image of God the Father. But this does not guarantee that bishops are preserved from all human weakness, even sin.

Receiving the Sacrament
of Holy Orders

Para. 1579–1582

Who may receive the Sacrament of Holy Orders? Except for deacons, the norm for receiving the Sacrament, according to the *Catechism*, is a man of faith living a celibate life.

Why celibacy? So that priests can serve Christ and His Church with an undivided heart. The *Catechism* assures us, "Accepted with a joyous heart celibacy radiantly proclaims the Reign of God."

In the Eastern Church, married men may be ordained as priests, but not as bishops. Celibacy, however, is held in great honor in the Eastern Church, and many priests freely choose it. Both the East and the West, however, hold that a man who has already received Holy Orders can no longer marry.

The ordained priest is of Christ, the *Catechism* says, and the Sacrament of Holy Orders "confers an *indelible spiritual character* and cannot be repeated nor conferred temporarily."

One Man and One Woman

Why does the Catholic Church insist that marriage can only be between one man and one woman? One has only to read the *Catechism* to understand the Church's reasoning regarding the tradition, purpose, and beauty of marriage as divined by its Creator.

God created man out of love, the *Catechism* reminds us, thus calling us to love. Love is the fundamental and innate vocation of every human being. The mutual love between man and woman becomes an image of the absolute and unfailing love with which God loves man.

God commanded Adam and Eve to "be fruitful and multiply and fill the earth." When a sexual act is closed to the gift of life, this command cannot be fulfilled.

The Sacrament of Marriage

The arguments raging in today's society as to the state of marriage and who may enter into it shouldn't cause us to forget its permanent characteristics.

According to the *Catechism*, the matrimonial covenant has two main purposes: "the good of the spouses and the procreation and education of offspring." Our Lord Jesus raised this covenant to the dignity of a Sacrament.

The *Catechism* also reminds us of the indisputable fact that marriage is not a purely human institution. God Himself is the Author of marriage, and only God, not man, can change its common and permanent characteristics. It began with the creation of man and woman in the image and likeness of God, who is love. Thus, their mutual and unfailing love becomes an image of the absolute and unfailing love with which God loves man.

The Bond of Marriage
Para. 1606–1608

"So they are no longer two, but one flesh." Nothing illustrates the powerful bond between man and wife intended by God, the Creator of marriage, than these words from Matthew's Gospel.

A true marriage is a sacramental bond and is therefore indissoluble. The *Catechism*, however, realistically acknowledges that the presence of evil can severely strain this bond. The marital union "has always been threatened by discord, a spirit of domination, infidelity, jealousy, and conflicts that can escalate into hatred and separation."

The original communion of Adam and Eve was ruptured by their sin of disobedience. "Their relations were distorted by mutual recriminations," says the *Catechism*, and brought about the pain of childbirth and the toil of work.

Without God's help, "man and woman cannot achieve the union of their lives for which God created them 'in the beginning.'"

History of Marriage

What is the origin of marriage? The *Catechism* tells us that God the Father instituted the marital union with our first parents, Adam and Eve. He clearly established it as a covenant between a man and a woman when He commanded them to be "fruitful and multiply."

Moses allowed divorce because of the hardness of his peoples' hearts, but when Jesus came, He restored the original order as planned by His Father. He declared that a true marriage was indissoluble: "What therefore God has joined together, let no man put asunder."

The *Catechism* states that the Church attaches great importance to the fact that Jesus' first miracle occurred at a wedding, signaling henceforth that "marriage will be an efficacious sign of Christ's presence."

An Impossible Demand?

Para. 1614–1616

Is it impossible to live Jesus Christ's command that the marriage bond be indissoluble? No, says the *Catechism*.

The Lord has not placed too heavy a burden on the shoulders of a married couple. "By coming to restore the original order of creation disturbed by sin, [Christ] himself gives the strength and grace to live marriage in the new dimension of the Reign of God. It is by following Christ, renouncing themselves, and taking up their crosses that spouses will be able to 'receive' the original meaning of marriage and live it with the help of Christ."

Saint Paul in his Letter to the Ephesians emphasizes this when he admonishes men to love their wives as Christ loved the Church. "For this reason," Paul says, "a man shall leave his father and mother and be joined to his wife, and the two shall become one."

Virginity for the Sake of the Kingdom

Para. 1618–1620

Why does the Catholic Church value virginity? At the heart and center of all Christian life is Christ the Lord. The *Catechism* tells us that our bond with Christ takes precedence over all bonds, familial or social.

From the Church's very beginning, there have been men and women who have forsaken marriage to follow the Lamb wherever He leads them. Christ Himself has invited certain persons to follow Him in this way of life for which He remains the model. "Virginity for the sake of the kingdom of heaven," the *Catechism* states, "is an unfolding of baptismal grace, a powerful sign of the supremacy of [a person's] bond with Christ."

It is also a sign that this bond recalls that marriage is a reality of this present age, which is passing away. Saint John Chrysostom puts it well: "The most excellent good is something even better than what is admitted to be good."

A Valid Marriage

Para. 1625–1628

What qualifies as a valid marriage in the eyes of the Catholic Church? The *Catechism* tells us there are certain requirements that must be present or the marriage is not a true Sacrament.

The requirements are as follows. The marriage must be between a baptized man and a baptized woman who are free to contract marriage and who freely express their consent. The *Catechism* defines freedom to contract as "not being under constraint" and "not impeded by any natural or ecclesiastical law." The exchange of consent between the spouses is considered by the Church to be the most indispensable element of a valid marriage.

According to the *Catechism*, "The consent must be an act of the will of each of the contracting parties, free of coercion or grave external fear. ... If this freedom is lacking the marriage is invalid."

Making Marriage a Visible Reality

Who may officiate at a wedding ceremony in the Catholic Church? According to the *Catechism*, in the Latin tradition, the Church's authorized ministers can be a priest or a deacon who presides over the ceremony and receives the consent of the two spouses in the name of the Church and gives them the blessing of the Church.

It is the presence of the ministers as well as the spouses that visibly expresses the fact that the marriage is an ecclesial reality.

The Church normally requires that the faithful contract marriage according to the ecclesiastical form because sacramental marriage is a liturgical act, so it ought to be celebrated in the public liturgy of the Church. Marriage is a state of life in the Church, so certainty about it is a necessity.

Preparation for marriage is of prime importance, says the *Catechism*, citing the example and teaching of parents and families as a special form of this preparation.

Conjugal Love

Para. 1643–1645

What does conjugal love entail? The *Catechism* tells us that conjugal love involves a totality of the whole person: the body, instinct, feeling, and affectivity as well as aspiration of the spirit and the will. "It aims at a deeply personal unity, a unity that, beyond union in one flesh, leads to forming one heart and soul."

Such a union demands faithfulness and indissolubility in definitive mutual self-giving and openness to fertility.

Polygamy is forbidden because each partner must be afforded equal personal dignity in mutual and unreserved affection. Polygamy, points out the *Catechism*, "is contrary to conjugal love which is undivided and exclusive."

The Fidelity of Conjugal Love

Para. 1643–1651

Why does marriage require complete fidelity between spouses? The *Catechism* states that the intimate union of marriage is a mutual self-giving of two persons ordered to the welfare of their children, which requires that there be an unbreakable union between them.

The deepest reason is found in the fidelity of Christ to His Church. Through the Sacrament of Matrimony, the spouses are able to represent that fidelity and witness to it. For these reasons, the spouses can be nothing but completely faithful to one another. Marriage is such a personal, deep union of giving oneself to the other that it cannot, the *Catechism* asserts, be an arrangement "until further notice."

As difficult as it may seem to retain this indissolubility for a lifetime, it is made possible by God's irrevocable love in which the couple shares, and which will support them through their marital journey.

Divorce and the Church

Para. 1650

What does the *Catechism* teach about divorce? The Church does not permit divorce in a valid marriage, because she is firmly adhering to the rules set down by her Founder.

Jesus Christ made it very clear that a sacramental, valid marriage was not to be dissolved. "Whoever divorces his wife and marries another," He declares, commits adultery against her; "and if she divorces her husband and marries another, she commits adultery" (Mark 10:11–12). Therefore, the Church maintains, a second marriage cannot be recognized as valid, if the first marriage is valid.

The *Catechism* tells us, "If the divorced are remarried civilly, they find themselves in a situation that objectively contravenes God's law." In such a situation, they may not receive Eucharistic Communion as long as this situation persists.

How Does the Catholic Church Treat Divorced Members?

Para. 1651

How does the Catholic Church treat divorced Catholics who have remarried outside the Church?

The *Catechism* tells us that the Catholic community must give "attentive solicitude" to Catholics who are divorced and remarried in a civil ceremony "so that they do not consider themselves separated from the Church, in whose life they can and must participate as baptized persons." Since their remarriage is against the command of Jesus, they may not receive Communion.

But, the *Catechism* says, "They should be encouraged to listen to the Word of God, to attend the Sacrifice of the Mass, to persevere in prayer ... to bring up their children in the Christian faith, to cultivate the spirit and practice of penance and thus implore, day by day, God's grace."

Thus, it follows, if a friend or family member marries outside the Church, we do not abandon them to no faith or another faith. We encourage them to remain a member of the Church's family.

The Crowning Glory of Marriage

Para. 1652–1654

What is the crowning glory of marriage? Marriage begins, the *Catechism* tells us, with two people who are, hopefully, very much in love. But by its very nature, it must be open to new life.

"Children are the supreme gift of marriage," the *Catechism* asserts, "and contribute greatly to the good of the parents themselves." God made it clear that it was not good for man to be alone, which is why He gave man a woman. Male and female He made them, Scripture tells us. Married love is ordered to the procreation and the education of offspring, and it is in them, the *Catechism* says, that marriage "finds its crowning glory."

Spouses to whom God has not granted children can nevertheless have a tangible life full of meaning, both in human and Christian terms. "Their marriage can radiate a fruitfulness of charity, of hospitality, and of sacrifice," the *Catechism* states.

Sacramentals

What are sacramentals, and how do they differ from the Sacraments?

The *Catechism* says they are sacred signs instituted by the Church. They prepare the faithful to receive the fruit of the Sacraments and they sanctify different circumstances of life. Blessings top the list in importance.

Blessings praise God and pray for His gifts and works and also convey the Church's intercession for the faithful in order that the faithful may use those gifts according to the will and the spirit of the Gospel. In addition, Christian life is nourished by various forms of popular piety.

While far less important than the Liturgy, these practices and devotions can, nevertheless, enrich Christian life.

Death of a Loved One

Para. 1681–1690

There is genuine consolation from the *Catechism* regarding the death of a loved one. The Christian who dies in Christ Jesus, we are told, is "away from the body and at home with the Lord." Death marks the end of a Christian's sacramental life, but the fulfillment of his new birth which began at Baptism and now has a definitive conformity to the image of Jesus Christ.

The Christian funeral does not give the deceased a Sacrament or sacramentals. The Christian funeral is a liturgical celebration of the Church and "the proclamation of eternal life to the community."

The greatest consolation to the Christian is the knowledge that, even in death, we are separated only temporarily — that, one day, if we have lived well, we will all be together again in Christ.

PART THREE:

LIFE IN CHRIST

Divine Glory Within

Para. 1691–1698

Did you know you have divine glory living within you?

If you are a baptized Christian you are host to a "gentle guest," says the *Catechism*, "a gentle guest and friend who inspires, guides, corrects, and strengthens" us to live our life in Christ. That gentle friend is the Spirit of Christ, the third person of the Blessed Trinity, the Holy Spirit. He is alive in us, transforming us spiritually, if we are willing, so that we may live as "children of light."

There are two ways to live. The first way, the way of Christ, leads to life. The opposite way leads to death, an eternity without God.

Choose life! Choose Christ, a life of challenge and joy.

The Life of Christ

What is "catechesis," and why do we care?

The job of catechesis is to reveal all the joy as well as the demands of the Way of Christ, says the *Catechism*. The Way of Christ is summed up in the catechesis of the Beatitudes.

Jesus gave us the eight Beatitudes in His Sermon on the Mount. The *Catechism* tells us this teaching is the only path that leads to the eternal beatitude — happiness — for which the human heart longs.

The catechesis of sin and forgiveness challenges us. "Unless man acknowledges that he is a sinner," states the *Catechism*, "he cannot know the truth about himself, which is a condition for acting justly; and without the offer of forgiveness he would not be able to bear this truth."

Man's Vocation

Para. 1700–1701

How does man fulfill his vocation? Through life in the Holy Spirit, the *Catechism* tells us. This life is made up of divine charity and human solidarity and is offered as salvation.

Man's great dignity is "rooted in his creation in the image and likeness of God" and "fulfilled in his vocation to divine beatitude." It is by our own actions, doing good and avoiding evil — freely chosen acts — that man conforms to the good promised by God.

"Human beings make their own contribution to their interior growth," the *Catechism* tells us. With the help of grace, man can avoid sin and grow in virtue.

It is Christ who reveals the mystery of the Father and His love for man, thus making man fully manifest to himself and bringing to light his exalted vocation.

We are Destined for Greatness

Para. 1701–1709

We were made for spiritual greatness. "The divine image is present in every man," the *Catechism* states, however dimly seen in some.

God gave man a spiritual and immortal soul. From the first moment in the womb, he or she is destined for eternal life with God. Man, by his reasoning, is capable of understanding the order the Creator has established. By our will, we are capable of aligning ourselves with our true good, which is where we find our perfection.

"By his reason, man recognizes the voice of God which urges him 'to do what is good and avoid what is evil,'" the *Catechism* says. The law of God is made known by our conscience, and is fulfilled by love of God and love of neighbor.

Because our first parents sinned, we suffer the wound of original sin. Thus, while we still desire good, we are inclined toward evil and subject to error.

Our Vocation to Beatitude

Para. 1716–1717

Webster's Dictionary defines "beatitude" first as a "state of utmost bliss," and second as "a declaration made in the Sermon on the Mount."

The *Catechism* defines the eight Beatitudes as, in effect, a portrait of the Man who declared them — Jesus Christ, saying they "depict [his] countenance ... and portray his charity." They also define the attitudes and the actions that should portray and depict the true Christian follower of Christ.

They are paradoxical in their promise that there is hope amid trial and tribulation — none more paradoxical than the eighth Beatitude, "Blessed are you when men revile you and persecute you and utter all kinds of evil against you falsely on my account. Rejoice and be glad for your reward is great in heaven."

What Makes You Happy?

Para. 1718–1720

What makes you happy? Truly and completely happy? Not for a day, or a week — what makes you happy day in, year out? Saint Thomas Aquinas says, "God alone satisfies."

We all, each and every one of us in the human category, desire happiness. Our Creator cleverly implanted that desire in our DNA, so that we would be drawn to Him who alone can fulfill that desire. The Beatitudes respond to our desire for happiness, because they reveal the ultimate end of human acts.

"God calls us to his own beatitude," according to the *Catechism*, variously characterized as the "coming of the Kingdom of God," "the vision of God," "the joy of the Lord," and "entering into God's rest."

Christian Beatitudes

Para. 1720–1724

What will eternal happiness (beatitude) be like? Saint Augustine has a pleasant description: "There we shall rest and see, we shall see and love, we shall love and praise. Behold what will be at the end without end. For what other end do we have, if not to reach the kingdom which has no end?"

The *Catechism* tells us, "God put us in the world to know, to love, and to serve him, and so to come to paradise." The Beatitudes present us with clear moral choices. We are invited to avoid evil, to purify our hearts of evil, and to love God above all earthly things, none of which can bring lasting happiness.

Lasting happiness can be found only in God who is the source of every good and all love.

Freedom
Para. 1730–1738

Frequently the question is asked: "Why is there evil in the world?" The answer resides in one word: Freedom. How can anything so good as freedom bring about so much bad?

Our Creator, the *Catechism* tells us, willed that "man be 'left in the hand of his own counsel.'" God created humans as rational beings, giving us the dignity to initiate and control our own actions in order that we might seek the Lord of our own accord and attain perfection by cleaving to Him.

The *Catechism* defines freedom as "the power, rooted in reason and will, to act or not to act, to do this or that, and so to perform deliberate actions on one's own responsibility." It is through free will that one shapes one's own life — to choose between good and evil.

The more good one does, the freer one becomes.

The Right to Exercise Freedom
Para. 1731–1738

How does freedom affect our actions? According to the *Catechism*, freedom makes us responsible for every act we have directly willed.

Despite her efforts to place all the blame on the serpent, Eve was directly responsible for initiating and committing original sin. She knew God had forbidden her to eat from the Tree of Good and Evil, yet she did it anyway.

Cain deliberately killed his brother Abel. David deliberately committed both adultery and murder.

None of the three were ignorant of the gravity of their acts, and there were no mitigating circumstances that diminished their responsibility. However, David was particularly remorseful when confronted with his guilt.

The *Catechism* tells us that *"the right to the exercise of freedom*, especially in moral and religious matters, is an inalienable requirement of the dignity of the human person."

Freedom and Grace

Para. 1739–1742

It is for our freedom that Christ has set us free, St. Paul tells the Galatians and us. In no way is the grace Christ won for us in competition with our freedom, the *Catechism* tells us. Rather, it enhances it, by promoting greater inner freedom when we conform our will to the true and the good that God has placed in our human hearts.

As this inner freedom grows, we are conditioned to face the trials and pressures visited upon us by the world in which we live.

"By the working of grace," says the *Catechism*, "the Holy Spirit educates us in spiritual freedom in order to make us free collaborators in his work in the Church and in the world."

Human Freedom
in the Economy of Salvation
Para. 1739–1742

Man failed the first test of freedom. He refused God's plan of love and chose freely to sin, and made himself a slave to sin. The first sin deprived mankind of the life-giving Holy Spirit, resulting in the inner disorder and inclination to sin which has given birth to numerous other sins.

The *Catechism* reminds us that "the exercise of freedom does not imply a right to say or do everything." Man is not totally self-sufficient, and his final goal is not his own self-interest and the enjoyment of earthly goals.

When man violates the moral law, he becomes his own prisoner, disrupting neighborly fellowships while rebelling against divine truth.

"For freedom," St. Paul's Letter to the Galatians tells us, "Christ has set us free." He redeemed us from sin, which held man in bondage.

The Morality of Human Acts

Para. 1749–1754

What makes an act moral or immoral? The *Catechism* lays out specific criteria for us to follow: "When he acts deliberately, man is, so to speak, the *father of his acts*. Human acts, that is, acts that are freely chosen in consequence of a judgment of conscience, can be morally evaluated. They are either good or evil."

The sources on which the morality of an act are determined are three: (1) the object chosen, (2) the intent of the act, and (3) the circumstances surrounding the act.

To be moral, the object of the act itself must be good and the intention pure. The circumstances are secondary to the first two criteria. They can increase or diminish the morality of the act. For instance: stealing a candy bar is wrong but far less evil than robbing a bank. Intent and circumstance, however, cannot change the moral quality of the act itself.

The end does not justify the means.

Good Acts and Evil Acts

Para. 1755–1756

The *Catechism* tells us that an evil end can corrupt an objectively good act. Our Lord pointed this out when He spoke of Pharisees praying and fasting — both objectively good acts — in order to be seen by men, a morally corrupt end that therefore corrupts all the actions.

On the other hand, a good intention cannot justify an objectively evil action. One cannot turn fornication — a morally evil action in and of itself — by participating in it, even to save a relationship. Fornication is always wrong because it involves a disorder of the will — a moral evil.

It is an error, the *Catechism* tells us, "to judge the morality of human acts by considering only the intention that inspires them or the circumstances (environment, social pressure, duress or emergency, etc.)."

The end never justifies the means.

Passion

Para. 1762–1770

What comes to mind when you hear the word "passion"? Passion often signifies an intensity of emotions and feelings — frequently in terms of lust.

But the *Catechism* tells us passions are neither good nor bad in and of themselves: "Passions are morally good when they contribute to a good action, evil in the opposite case."

The most fundamental passion is love, says the *Catechism*. It is aroused by attraction to the good, the desire to attain the good, and fulfilled by joy and pleasure once the good is possessed. Evil, on the other hand, arouses hatred, aversion, and fear.

Passions are the passageway connecting the senses and the mind. Jesus said the source of all passions was the human heart.

Conscience
Para. 1776–1778

How do we listen to God? Contrary to popular opinion that God only speaks to the privileged few, the *Catechism* reminds us that He communicates to all of us, through our conscience.

On our hearts, in our most secret core, God has inscribed the moral law. This law calls man to live and to do what is good and avoid evil. In the aloneness of the sanctuary that is our conscience, our Creator's voice echoes in our depths.

"When he listens to his conscience," says the *Catechism*, "the prudent man can hear God speaking."

Conscience is a judgment of reason whereby the human person recognizes the moral quality of a concrete act about to perform, is already performing, or has already been performed. Saint John Henry Cardinal Newman defined conscience as "a law of the mind" whereby God "speaks to us behind a veil."

The Voice of Our Conscience

Para. 1776–1782

How do we recognize the voice of our conscience? The *Catechism* says that in order to discern exactly what our conscience is telling us about a contemplated action, every person must be sufficiently present to himself in order to hear and follow his conscience.

Saint Augustine says, "Return to your conscience, question it. Turn inward, brethren, and in everything you do, see God as your witness."

Conscience empowers us to assume responsibility for an act committed. "Man has the right to act in conscience and in freedom so as to personally make moral decisions," asserts the *Catechism*. "He must not be forced to act contrary to his conscience. Nor must he be prevented from acting according to his conscience, especially in religious matters."

Formation of Conscience

Para. 1783–1785

How does a well-formed conscience behave? In order to make correct moral judgments, we must have a well-formed conscience that is upright and truthful and formulates judgments according to reason. The *Catechism* tells us to conform those judgments to the true good, willed by the wisdom of the Creator.

In short, a good conscience enables one to act according to the will of God. In order to avoid the trap of negative influences and the tendency to prefer our own judgments, we must educate our conscience. The *Catechism* promises that "prudent education teaches virtue; it prevents or cures fear, selfishness, and pride," and "guarantees freedom and engenders peace of heart."

What are the ingredients of this educational stew? One is the Word of God, which we absorb through faith and prayer. Two, we must "examine our conscience before the Lord's Cross."

The *Catechism* concedes that our modern world can make discernment difficult, but it tells us we must always seek what is right and what is the will of God, as expressed in divine law.

Erroneous Judgments

Are we always obliged to obey our conscience? It depends on what kind of a conscience we have.

The *Catechism* tells us that "a human being must always obey the certain judgment of his conscience." If we deliberately act against such a conscience, we condemn ourselves.

On the other hand, our moral conscience may reside in ignorance, and thus we are subject to erroneous judgments about acts in the future or those performed in the past. If one is personally responsible for one's ignorance, one is still culpable of the sin one commits.

What are the causes of erroneous judgment? The *Catechism* lists several: ignorance of Christ and His Gospel, the bad example of others, enslavement to one's passions, rejection of the Church's authority and her teaching, and lack of conversion and charity.

The Virtues

Para. 1804

What is a virtue? According to the *Catechism*, a virtue is a habitual and firm disposition to do the good, enabling a person not just to perform good acts, but to give the best of himself or herself.

The goal of the virtuous life is to become like God. "*Human virtues* are firm attitudes, stable dispositions, [and] habitual perfections of intellect and will that govern our actions," says the *Catechism*. A virtuous person has mastery over him- or herself and takes joy in leading a morally good life.

Acquired through human effort, the moral virtues are the seed and fruit of morally good acts, disposing us to communion with divine love.

The Virtue of Fortitude

Para. 1808

What keeps us standing when all around us is falling? It is fortitude, one of the four cardinal virtues.

The *Catechism* describes fortitude as "the moral virtue that ensures firmness in difficulties and constancy in the pursuit of the good." When temptation confronts us, it is the shield of fortitude that helps protect us against surrender.

Fortitude helps us overcome moral obstacles and even the fear of death. It provides us the strength to face trials and persecutions. It even disposes us to sacrifice our own life, if necessary, in pursuit of a just cause.

In John 16:33, Jesus bolsters our fortitude with these words: "In the world, you will have tribulations, but be of good cheer, I have overcome the world."

Temperance

We hear a lot about the virtue of temperance in regard to alcoholic consumption. In reality, temperance is to be exercised in regard to all pleasures at all times.

The *Catechism* defines temperance as "the moral virtue that moderates the attraction of pleasures and provides balance in the use of created goods." It ensures mastery of the will over our instincts, and keeps our desires within honorable limits.

The Old Testament praises temperance by cautioning us against following our base desires and urging us to restrain our appetites, which could mean forgoing that second chocolate-chip cookie.

The New Testament puts it this way: "We ought to live sober, upright and godly lives in this world," helping us on the road to a desirable location in the next.

Acquiring the Virtues

Para. 1810–1811

How do we acquire virtue? The *Catechism* advises that human virtues can be acquired by deliberate acts, by perseverance, and through education. They are, however, purified and elevated by divine grace.

Because of the wounds inflicted by sin, it is not easy for man to maintain moral balance. But Christ's gift of salvation offers us the grace necessary to continue pursuing the virtues.

"Everyone," points out the *Catechism*, "should always ask for this grace of light and strength, frequent the sacraments, cooperate with the Holy Spirit, and follow his calls to love what is good and shun evil."

The Theological Virtues and Faith

What are the theological virtues? The *Catechism* tells us they are the foundation of Christian moral activity. Infused into our souls by God, they enable us to act as God's children and merit eternal life.

The three theological virtues are faith, hope, and charity. Faith is the virtue by which we believe in God and all that He has said and revealed to us, as well as what the Church has proposed for our belief, because God is truth itself. The Apostle James, however, reminds us that faith without works is dead.

A disciple of Christ, says the *Catechism*, must also be willing to profess and spread the faith, which is necessary for salvation. Our Lord put it strongly: "So every one who acknowledges me before men, I will acknowledge before my Father who is in heaven; but whoever denies me before men, I also will deny before my Father who is in heaven."

Hope

Para. 1817–1821

Remember the song, "You Gotta Have Heart"? One of the lines is, "You gotta have hope." Well, it's not *all* you need, but it *is* one of the three theological virtues.

The *Catechism* tells us that hope helps us desire Heaven and eternal life as our happiness. We trust in Jesus' promise, while relying, not just on our own strengths, but the assistance extended by grace from the Holy Spirit.

Hope keeps discouragement at bay and sustains us in times of abandonment. It preserves us from selfishness by leading us to the happiness that flows from charity. Christian hope unfolds from Jesus' preaching of the Beatitudes, which raises our hope to Heaven as the new Promised Land.

"Hope is expressed and nourished in prayer," the *Catechism* says, "especially in the Our Father, the summary of everything that hope leads us to desire."

Charity
Para. 1822–1829

Love makes the world go round, songwriters tell us. But there is a greater love than mere romantic love.

The theological virtue of love, called charity, means we love God above all things, for His own sake, just because He's God and infinitely loveable. We love our neighbor as ourselves because we love God and He desires us to love our neighbor.

The *Catechism* tells us that Jesus makes charity the "new commandment." By loving His own to the end, Jesus renders the Father's love — which He receives — visible.

While we were yet in our sins — as such, His enemies — Christ died out of love for us. He asks us to love as He does. Love even our enemies. Make even those far from us our neighbors. Love children and the poor as Christ Himself.

Saint Augustine writes, "Love is itself the fulfillment of all our works. There is the goal; that is why we run toward it, and once we reach it [love], in it we shall find rest."

The Gifts and Fruits of the Holy Spirit

Para. 1830–1832

The Gifts of the Holy Spirit are "permanent dispositions which make man docile in following the promptings of the Holy Spirit," according to the *Catechism*. These gifts sustain the moral life of the Christian.

There are seven gifts: wisdom, understanding, counsel, fortitude, knowledge, piety, and fear of the Lord (commonly known today as "awe and wonder"). Those who are led by the Spirit of God are children and heirs of God, co-heirs with Christ in whom the gifts are seen in their fullness.

The Fruits of the Holy Spirit are 12 in number: charity, joy, peace, patience, kindness, goodness, generosity, gentleness, faithfulness, modesty, self-control, and chastity. The *Catechism* explains that the fruits are "perfections that the Holy Spirit forms in us as the first fruits of eternal glory."

Mercy and Sin
Para. 1846–1850

What is God's most amazing quality? Surely it must be His enormous mercy toward sinners. This mercy is revealed in the Gospel through Jesus Christ.

Jesus' very Name means salvation for sinners, says the *Catechism*. The Eucharist is the Sacrament of redemption.

There is a condition to God's mercy, however, and that is our knowledge and admission that we indeed have sinned and are in need of His mercy. If we say we have no sin, we deceive ourselves, the Gospel of John reminds us. But if we confess our guilt, God will mercifully cleanse us of all unrighteousness.

Pope St. John Paul II asserted that "conversion requires convincing of sin." So, just as a physician must probe a wound before treating it, God through His Word and His Spirit casts a living light on sin. But along with the sting of conscience comes the salve of the certainty of redemption, so the Holy Spirit is both surgeon and consoler.

Sin

Para. 1849–1851

How do we define sin? The *Catechism* defines it in detail, calling sin "an offense against reason, truth, and right conscience; it is failure in genuine love for God and neighbor caused by a perverse attachment to certain goods."

Saint Augustine defined sin as an utterance, a deed, or a desire contrary to the eternal law. Sin is an offense against God, as King David lamented in Psalm 51: "Against you, you alone, have I sinned and done that which is evil in your sight."

We sin when we love ourselves even to the extent of having contempt of God. The *Catechism* points out that sin in its most ugly forms is exercised against Christ during the Passion. Ironically, at this darkest hour, the light of Christ's sacrifice becomes the inexhaustible source for the forgiveness of sin.

Mortal Sin
Para. 1854–1861

There are many kinds of sin, but not all sins are equal, the *Catechism* teaches. The gravity of a sin is distinguished according to its object, or to the virtue it opposes or the commandment it violates.

The root of sin lies within the human heart, Jesus declared. "For out of the heart some evil thoughts: murder, adultery, fornication, theft, false witness, slander," warned the Lord. "These are what defile a man." But charity, the source of all good works, also resides in the heart. The gravest sin — mortal sin — destroys that charity by a serious violation of God's law.

To commit a mortal sin, the object must be grave. There must be full knowledge of that gravity and full consent of the will. If not repented and forgiven by God, mortal sin can exclude us from Christ's Kingdom and merit "the eternal death of hell," for, as the *Catechism* reminds us, "our freedom has the power to make choices for ever, with no turning back."

Proliferation of Sin

Para. 1865–1869

"Sin creates a proclivity to sin," the *Catechism* teaches. It develops vice by repetition of the same wrong act. Thus sin tends to reinforce and reproduce itself.

Vice can be linked to the capital sins, which are called "capital" because they can engender other sins and other vices.

The capital sins, also known as the seven deadly sins, are pride, avarice, envy, wrath, lust, gluttony, and sloth.

Sin is a personal act, but we can also be responsible for the sins of others under certain conditions. "Sin makes men accomplices of one another," the *Catechism* warns, "and causes concupiscence, violence, and injustice to reign among them."

The Human Community

Para. 1877–1879

Ever wonder why social networking is such a popular internet exercise? We humans are hardwired for society. It's in our DNA.

"The human person needs to live in society," the *Catechism* tells us. It is a requirement of his nature. There is a certain resemblance between the unity of the three Divine Persons and the fraternity that humans are to establish among themselves in truth and love. As Jesus made clear, love of God is inseparable from love of neighbor.

Humanity's vocation, says the *Catechism*, is "to show forth the image of God and to be transformed into the image of the Father's only Son," Jesus. Through mutual service and dialogue with one another we develop our potential and thus respond to the end to which we are called: God Himself.

Vocation of Humanity

Para. 1877–1885

What is humanity's vocation? According to the *Catechism*, "The vocation of humanity is to show forth the image of God and to be transformed into the image of the Father's only Son," Jesus Christ.

God is the end to which all men are called. The *Catechism* says there is a certain resemblance between the fraternal union that human beings are to establish among themselves and the divine union of the Holy Trinity in truth and love.

Love of neighbor is inseparable from love of God. We humans need society. Society is not an add-on for us but a requirement of our nature. Through our exchange with others, mutual service, and dialogue with our brothers and sisters, we develop our potential and thus respond to our vocation.

What Is a Society?

Para. 1878–1885

What composes society? The *Catechism* says human beings need to live in society. It is there that we develop our potential.

The *Catechism* defines a society as "a group of persons bound together organically by a principle of unity that goes beyond each one of them." A society endures through time.

We owe loyalty to the communities that we are part of, which are defined by their purpose. All social institutions, however, ought to have the human person as its principle, subject, and end. The societies of family and state are necessary to the nature of man. Other societies, such as voluntary associations and institutions, are encouraged for economic, cultural, athletic, and professional reasons. The Church warns against certain types of socialization wherein excessive intervention of the state threatens personal freedom and initiative.

Government and Individual Rights

Para. 1883–1885

How does God's method of governing provide a role model for governors of human communities? God is a delegator. He has not, the *Catechism* points out, "willed to reserve to himself all exercise of power. He entrusts to every creature the functions it is capable of performing, according to the capacities of its own nature."

God displays great regard for human freedom. Inspired by God, human governors should behave as instruments of Divine Providence and practice the "principle of subsidiarity," which ordains that "a community of a higher order should not interfere in the internal life of a community of a lower order, depriving the latter of its functions."

The *Catechism* stresses that the principle of subsidiarity sets limits on state intervention. The collective ends of society can never justify using means that trample individual rights.

The Necessity of Society

Para. 1886–1896

How should society and the soul interact? According to the *Catechism,* "Society is essential to the fulfillment of the human vocation. To attain this aim, respect must be accorded to the just hierarchy of values," which places interior and spiritual dimensions above physical and instinctual ones.

In other words, society ought, the *Catechism* states, to "promote the exercise of virtue, not obstruct it." The end can never justify the means. If means become ends rather than routes to spiritual goals, the human person in society can become a utilitarian object.

Unjust structures can be created that make Christian conduct in keeping the commandments of the Divine lawgiver difficult or impossible to follow.

Responsibility and Participation in Society

Para. 1913–1915

How serious is our responsibility to participate in furthering the common good? Very serious. According to the *Catechism*, "'Participation' is the voluntary and generous engagement of a person in social interchange. ... This obligation is inherent in the dignity of the human person."

Participation calls, first of all, for us to be conscientious in exercising our responsibility in areas where we are directly involved: our families, our children's education, and our work.

"As far as possible," the *Catechism* urges, "citizens should take an active part in *public life*." This leads to the *Catechism*'s conclusion that nations that allow the broadest possible citizen participation are the nations to be lauded.

The Common Good

Para. 1924–1927

What do we mean by "the common good"? The common good, as defined by the *Catechism*, is "the sum total of social conditions which allow people, either as groups or as individuals, to reach their fulfillment more fully and more easily."

The common good concerns the life of all. It consists of three essential elements:

- Respect for the person as such. Authorities are bound to respect the fundamental and inalienable rights of the human person.
- Social well-being, which means making accessible what is needed to lead a truly human life.
- Peace, meaning the stability and security of a just order.

"It is the role of the state to defend and promote the common good of civil society," the *Catechism* states. International organizations are needed to promote the good of the whole human family.

Social Justice

Para. 1929–1931

What does the Church mean when she speaks of social justice? The *Catechism* says society ensures social justice when it allows associations and individuals to obtain their due.

Social justice can only be accomplished by respecting the transcendent dignity of man. In other words, society exists for man. Man does not exist for society.

"The person," says the *Catechism*, "represents the ultimate end of society, which is ordered to him." By refusing to recognize the inherent rights of the individual as endowed by the Creator, a society undermines its own moral legitimacy, according to Pope St. John XXIII.

Respect for the human person stems from the principle that everyone should look upon his neighbor as another self.

Equality and Differences
Among Human Beings

Para. 1934–1938

Human beings are equal and different at the same time.

The *Catechism* teaches that all persons are created in the image of God. They are equally endowed with rational souls and derived from the same origin. Having been redeemed by the same sacrifice of Christ on the Cross, they are all called to participate in the same beatitude. As such, they enjoy equal dignity as persons.

"Every form of social or cultural discrimination in fundamental personal rights on the grounds of sex, race, color, social conditions, language or religion must be curbed or eradicated as incompatible with God's design," the *Catechism* says.

Differences in mankind stem from physical, intellectual, and moral abilities. These differences are part of God's plan.

Since man is not equipped with everything he needs, God wills that he receive what he needs from others.

Sacred Scripture —
The Big Picture
Para. 1965–1974

Why is the "New Law" — the Law of the Gospel — called the Law of Love? It is so called because it helps us act out of love, infused by the Holy Spirit, rather than fear.

It is also called the Law of Grace, the *Catechism* tells us, because it gives us the strength to act by means of faith and the Sacraments.

A third name for the New Law is the Law of Freedom, because it frees us from the ritual and juridical observances of the old law. It prompts us to act spontaneously via the nudgings of charity. It allows us to move from servant to friend of Christ and even to son and heir.

"For all that I have heard from my Father," the Lord said, "I have made known to you."

The Call to Holiness —
To Perfection

Para. 2012–2016

We are all called to holiness — to be perfect as our Heavenly Father is perfect. How is this possible? Not by our own merits, but through the free gift of grace from God.

Our job is to cooperate with those graces. Spiritual progress, the *Catechism* tells us, tends toward ever more intimate union with Christ. Such a union is called a "mystical" union because it participates in the mysteries of Christ through the Sacraments, which are called "holy mysteries."

Intimate union with Christ brings us into the mystery of the Trinity. The *Catechism* warns us, "The way of perfection passes by way of the Cross. There is no holiness without renunciation and spiritual battle."

Saint Gregory of Nyssa said, "He who climbs never stops." In other words, for the true Christian, there are no endings, only new beginnings.

The First Commandment

What does God ask of us through the First Commandment? The *Catechism* tells us, "God's first call and just demand is that man accept him and worship him. ... 'Him only shall you serve.'"

God first revealed His glory to Israel. The truth of man and man's vocation is linked to this revelation of God.

What is man's vocation? It is to make God manifest by acting in conformity with the fact that man has been made in the image and likeness of God.

The source of our moral life is faith in God. Saint Paul writes that the principle and explanation of all moral deviation is ignorance of God.

The Virtues in the First Commandment

Para. 2084–2087

What three virtues are embodied in the First Commandment? The *Catechism* tells us that the First Commandment encompasses the three theological virtues: faith, hope, and charity.

In this commandment, God calls us to "worship the Lord your God and him only shall you serve." When we say "God," we confess our belief in a constant, unchangeable Being, always faithful and just, without evil. It naturally follows that we accept His words and thus have complete faith in Him.

"He is almighty, merciful, and infinitely beneficent," the *Catechism* states. "Who could not place all hope in him?"

Finally, who could not love a Creator who has poured out His love, His goodness, and His gifts on us?

Hope in the First Commandment

Hope is discussed in 12 different sections of the *Catechism*. In one section, the *Catechism* tells us that when God fully reveals Himself and calls man, man cannot fully respond on his own. "He must hope that God will give him the capacity to love Him in return and to act in conformity with the commandment of charity."

Hope confidently expects divine blessing and the beatific vision of God, while fearing to offend Him and incur punishment.

Despair is a sin against hope because, when a person despairs, he or she ceases to hope for eternal salvation, which denies God's goodness, justice, and mercy.

The sin of presumption, on the other hand, assumes God will give forgiveness without conversion and glory without merit, or presumes that man can win salvation with no supernatural assistance.

Charity in the First Commandment

Para. 2093–2094

How does the First Commandment encompass the virtue of charity? The *Catechism* says it commands us "to love God above everything and all creatures for him and because of him."

There are numerous ways to sin against God's love. The sin of indifference neglects or refuses to contemplate divine charity. Ingratitude refuses to even acknowledge divine charity or return to God love for love.

Lukewarmness is hesitation or negligence in responding to divine love. "Spiritual sloth" occurs when a person rejects the joy coming from God and is repelled by divine goodness.

Finally, actual hatred of God denies His goodness and curses Him as the One who forbids sin and inflicts punishments.

Adoration and Prayer

Para. 2096–2098

Why is adoration the first act of the virtue of religion? Because, says the *Catechism*, it acknowledges God as the Creator and Savior, the Master of everything that exists.

When we adore God, we, in all humility, admit our nothingness as the creature who would not even exist were it not for God. Worshiping God sets us free from the slavery of sin and idolatry of the world and from turning in on ourselves.

To adore God is to praise and exalt Him and to humble ourselves, as Mary did in her prayer, the Magnificat, confessing with gratitude that God has done great things and holy is His Name.

"Prayer," says the *Catechism*, "is an indispensable condition for being able to obey God's commandments." Jesus told His disciples they should pray always and never lose heart.

Sacrifice

Para. 2099–2100

Why is sacrifice an important part of worship? The *Catechism* tells us that it is right and good to offer sacrifice to God as a sign of adoration, gratitude, supplication, and communion.

What is the sacrifice most pleasing to God? Psalm 51 says, "It is a broken spirit." What does that mean?

The *Catechism* counsels that "outward sacrifice, to be genuine, must be the expression of spiritual sacrifice." Old Covenant prophets denounced sacrifices that were not from the heart, or not coupled with love of neighbor.

The one perfect sacrifice was Jesus' agony and death on the Cross. By uniting ourselves with the Lord's sacrifice, we can make our lives a sacrifice to God.

Promises and Vows

In the world of religion, what constitutes a promise? What constitutes a vow? How do they differ?

The *Catechism* states that the Christian is called to make promises in a number of different ways, such as in the Sacraments of Baptism, Confirmation, Matrimony, and Holy Orders. A Christian may also make promises that are uniquely his own, such as promising to say certain prayers, give alms, or make a pilgrimage.

Remaining faithful to a promise we make to God demonstrates the respect due Him and His divine love.

A vow is a deliberate and free act of devotion in which a Christian dedicates himself to God or promises God some good work. The Church recognizes as especially exemplary those who vow to embrace the evangelical counsels of poverty, chastity, and obedience.

Idolatry

Para. 2112–2114

What is idolatry? Idolatry is the worship of false gods. The *Catechism* tells us that Scripture constantly recalls the rejection of idols such as silver and gold fashioned by men's hands. Such empty idols make those who worship them as empty and dead and lifeless as the idols they create.

The one true God, on the other hand, is the living God who gives life and who intervenes in history.

"Man commits idolatry whenever he honors and reveres a creature in place of God," the *Catechism* continues, "whether this be gods or demons (for example, satanism), power, pleasure, race, ancestors, the state, money, etc."

Jesus Christ warns us that we cannot serve both God and mammon.

Divination and Magic

Para. 2115–2117

What does the *Catechism* teach concerning the natural human curiosity and desire to know the future? It counsels us that "a sound Christian attitude consists in putting oneself confidently in the hands of Providence for whatever concerns the future, and giving up all unhealthy curiosity about it."

What does the *Catechism* condemn as unhealthy curiosity? All forms of "divination" — deifying objects as persons — are to be rejected, as are consulting horoscopes, astrology, palm readings, interpretations of omens and lots, clairvoyance, and mediums. All these venues conceal a desire for power over time, history, and other human beings — powers that belong to God alone.

Major Sins Against the
First Commandment

Para. 2118–2122

What are the three major sins against the First Commandment? The *Catechism* lists them as "tempting God," sacrilege, and simony.

How can we tempt God? By putting His goodness and almighty power to the test by word or deed, as Satan dared to do when he commanded that Jesus throw Himself down from the temple. He was trying to force God to act. Jesus rebuked the devil with God's Word: "You shall not put the Lord thy God to the test."

The sin of sacrilege profanes the Sacraments and other liturgical actions as well as persons, things, or places consecrated to God. It is particularly grave when committed against the Eucharistic Jesus.

Simony is the sin of buying and selling of spiritual blessings. It is named after Simon the magician, who attempted to purchase spiritual power from St. Peter.

Atheism

What is atheism? The *Catechism* calls atheism "'one of the most serious problems of our time.'"

Atheism, the rejection of the intimate bond between man and God, covers many very different phenomena such as practical materialism, which restricts man's needs to space and time. Another is secular humanism, which considers man to be an end to himself and in control of his own history.

A third form of atheism is liberation, which seeks to free man through economic and social liberation, claiming that religion, by its very nature, thwarts man's emancipation by holding that there is an after and better life, thus deceiving man and discouraging him from working for a better life here on earth.

The Second Commandment
Para. 2142–2159

Why does the Second Commandment forbid taking the Lord's Name in vain? "Among all the words of Revelation," the *Catechism* states, "there is one which is unique: the revealed name of God."

God discloses Himself in His personal mystery when He confides His name to those who believe in Him. Thus we are to keep God's Name in silent adoration with love, and only use it in our speech to praise, bless, and glorify Him.

Any other use of the Holy Name is an abuse. If we make a promise to another, using God's Name, it must be respected in justice. If we are unfaithful to such a promise, we make God out to be a liar.

Sins against the Second Commandment

Para. 2148–2155

Why are blasphemy, perjury, and the taking of a false oath sins against the Second Commandment? Because they are in direct contradiction to God's directive that we do not take His Name in vain.

Blasphemy, the *Catechism* explains, is "uttering against God — inwardly or outwardly — words of hatred, reproach, or defiance," as well as "speaking ill of God," "failing in respect toward him in one's speech," and "misusing God's name."

We commit perjury if we call upon God to witness an oath we do not intend to honor, or after swearing an oath, we fail to keep it. The *Catechism* states that when we take an oath and call on God as our witness, we invoke divine truthfulness as a pledge of our truthfulness.

The holiness of the Lord's Name demands that it never be used trivially or to witness to unholy authority.

No Work on the Sabbath?

Para. 2168–2188

Why should we do no work on the Sabbath, as the Third Commandment demands?

The *Catechism* reminds us that "in six days, the Lord made heaven and earth, the sea, and all that is in them, and rested the seventh day; therefore the Lord blessed the Sabbath day and hallowed it." The Sabbath is also a memorial of Israel's liberation from Egypt.

The Sabbath is a sign of God's irrevocable covenant with Israel. Thus the day is to be set apart as holy and for the praise of God, His work of Creation, and His saving action on behalf of Israel. God set a model for human action.

If the Almighty Creator could take a day off for rest and refreshment, so should His creatures.

For Christians, Sunday replaces Sabbath observance because it is the day Jesus rose from the dead and ushered in the New Creation.

Why Sunday?

Why does the Catholic Church obligate its members to attend Mass on Sundays?

For Christians, Sunday, the first day of the week or the "eighth day," replaces the seventh day, the Sabbath, as the day to reserve for worshiping God. The Sabbath represents the completion of the first creation.

When Jesus Christ arose from the dead on Sunday, He inaugurated the new creation. Thus, Sunday became the Lord's Day and is now the foremost holy day of obligation in the universal Church.

We are bound to attend Mass, under pain of grave sin, unless there is a serious reason for not doing so.

Sundays are also called to be a day of rest. Christians are bound to abstain from work, which impedes worshiping God and the joy of the Lord's Day.

First among the Commandments

When asked which Commandments were first in rank of importance, Jesus said,

> The first is, "Hear O Israel: The Lord our God, the Lord is one; and you shall love the Lord your God with all your heart, and with all your soul, and with all your mind and with all your strength." The second is this: "You shall love your neighbor as yourself." There is no other commandment greater than these. (Mk 12:29-31)

The *Catechism* quotes St. Paul as saying, "He who loves his neighbor has fulfilled the law." Why? If you love your neighbor, you will do him no harm. All the Commandments, says Paul, are involved in loving your neighbor as yourself. The Commandments forbidding adultery, murder, stealing, and coveting are summed up in that one sentence.

The Fourth Commandment

What is the essence of the Fourth Commandment? In ordering us to honor our mother and our father, the Lord God has willed that, after Him, we should revere our parents to whom we owe life and who have handed on to us the knowledge of God.

The *Catechism* says the Fourth Commandment shows us the order of charity. It introduces the subsequent Commandments concerned with special respect for life, marriage, earthly goods, and speech. It constitutes one of the foundations of the social doctrines of the Church.

It is expressed specifically to children regarding their relationship to their parents because it is the most universal, but it also involves ties of kinship to the extended family and encompasses duties to elders and ancestors, of pupils to teachers, of employees to employers, and of citizens to their country and to those who govern it.

Obedience to All in the Fourth Commandment

Does the Fourth Commandment only order us to honor our father and our mother? According to the *Catechism*, it also obliges us to "honor and respect all those whom God, for our good, has vested with his authority."

Respecting the Fourth Commandment, says the *Catechism*, brings its own reward: not only with spiritual fruits, but temporal benefits of peace and prosperity—whereas failure to observe the Commandment brings harm to individuals and communities.

We are reminded that marriage and the family are ordered to the good of the spouses and the procreation and education of children. The *Catechism* states, "A man and a woman united in marriage, together with their children, form a family."

God instituted the human family when He created man and woman and instructed them to "increase and multiply."

The Economy and Social Justice
Para. 2426–2436

How does the Catholic Church regard the economy and social justice? The *Catechism* states, "The development of economic activity and growth in production are meant to provide for the needs of human beings." Economic life "is ordered first of all to the service of persons, of the whole man, and of the entire human community."

Human work comes from persons who have been created in the image and likeness of their Creator, God, who commissions them to prolong the work of creation by subduing the earth both with and for one another.

Work is a duty, says the *Catechism*. Saint Paul writes, "If anyone will not work, let him not eat." Work honors the gifts and talents God has bestowed on His creatures. Work can be redemptive, when its hardships are placed in union with Jesus.

The Eighth Commandment
Para. 2464–2503

What does the Eighth Commandment demand of us? The *Catechism* says this commandment forbids misrepresenting the truth in our relations with others. This derives from the vocation of holy people to bear witness to their God, Who is truth and Who wills the truth.

Offenses against the truth, either by word or deed, are fundamental infidelities to God and thus undermine the foundation of our covenant with Him. The Old Testament tells us God is the source of all truth. His word is truth as well as law.

Jesus Christ is the whole of God's truth made manifest. To follow Christ "is to live in 'the Spirit of truth,'" says the *Catechism*.

Jesus taught His disciples the unequivocal nature of truth when He instructed them, "Let your 'Yes' mean 'Yes,' and your 'No' mean 'No.' Anything more is from the evil one" (Mt 5:37).

What Is Truth?

Para. 2465–2474

"What is truth?" Pontius Pilate asked Jesus, not realizing that he was looking *at* Truth. Jesus Christ *is* the truth and the source of all truth.

"Man tends by nature toward the truth," the *Catechism* states. "He is obliged to honor and bear witness to it." Saint Thomas Aquinas asserts, "Men could not live with one another if there were not mutual confidence that they were being truthful with one another."

Truth entails both honesty and discretion, between what ought to be expressed and what ought to be kept secret. Jesus told Pilate that He had come into the world to "bear witness to the truth." Thus, the *Catechism* states, "In situations that require witness to the faith, the Christian must profess it without equivocation," even at the sacrifice of their life.

Witnesses to the Truth

Para. 2471–2474

Do we the people in the pews have the responsibility to be witnesses to the Gospel in the way we act and speak? Yes, asserts the *Catechism*.

The *Catechism* defines witness as "an act of justice that establishes truth or makes it known." As a witness, we manifest the new person we have put on in Baptism and we reveal the power of the Holy Spirit that was strengthened in us through reception of Confirmation.

Martyrdom, says the *Catechism*, is the supreme witness to the truth given us through faith. Saint Ignatius of Antioch boldly proclaimed, "Let me become food of the beasts, through whom it will be given me to reach God." The *Catechism* hails martyrs who "form archives of truth written in letters of blood."

Offenses against the Eighth Commandment

Para. 2475–2478

What are some major offenses against the Eighth Commandment? The *Catechism* states that false witness — that is, lying in court — and perjury, which is lying under oath, are especially grave sins because they are stated publicly. Such false statements, the *Catechism* says, "contribute to the condemnation of the innocent, exoneration of the guilty, or the increased punishment of the accused."

If we assume the moral fault of another without sufficient evidence, we commit the sin of rash judgment. We offend by the sin of detraction when we reveal the faults of another, without an objectively valid reason, to someone who did not know them.

Calumny is the sin of lying about another person, thereby harming their reputation and contributing to occasions of false judgments regarding them.

Truth and Social Media

Para. 2493–2499

What responsibility does social media bear in promoting the truth?

The *Catechism* notes that, in our modern society, the communications media play a major role in societal information, cultural promotion, and formation. Since society has a right to information that is based on truth, justice, freedom, and solidarity, every segment of the communications culture bears a heavy responsibility for the common good. Media content within the bounds of justice and charity must be true and complete and communicated honestly and properly.

The *Catechism* cautions us to be "vigilant" rather than passive consumers of information in order to resist unwholesome influences. Journalists are urged to respect the facts, while still observing charity by not stooping to defamation of individuals.

The Beauty of Truth
Para. 2500–2503

What qualities are embodied in truth and goodness? The *Catechism* asserts that the practice of goodness is accompanied by the joy and splendor of spiritual beauty.

Truth, says the *Catechism*, is beautiful in and of itself. Because man is endowed with an intellect, truth in the rational expression of the created and the uncreated reality is necessary. But when truth is beyond words — the depths of the human heart, the exaltation of the soul, the mystery of God — other forms of complementary human expression are needed.

Before God revealed Himself in words, He revealed Himself in the universal language of creation — the order and harmony of the cosmos that both child and scientist can discern.

The Ninth Commandment and Concupiscence

Para. 2514–2527

What does the Ninth Commandment forbid? The *Catechism* says it warns against carnal concupiscence, or sins against the flesh.

Concupiscence — defined by St. John as lust of the flesh, lust of the eyes, and pride of life — is the consequence of original sin. Though Baptism purifies the soul of all sin, it does not remove our tendency toward sin.

In this rebellion of the flesh against the spirit, as defined by St. Paul, we must develop purity of heart — the desire always to do the will of God especially in the area of charity and chastity.

Purity requires modesty. Modesty protects the intimate center of a person. It refuses to unveil what should be hidden. Modesty guides how you look at others and behave toward them. It should dictate one's choice of clothing, so as not to exploit or tempt another.

The Tenth Commandment
Para. 2534–2540

What does the Tenth Commandment condemn? When the Lord God told us not to covet our neighbor's goods, He denounced envy, avarice, and greed as the root of theft, robbery, and fraud.

Greed, the *Catechism* tells us, is the desire to amass earthly goods without limit. Avarice arises from a passion for riches and the power that attends to their possession. He who loves money never has money enough, says the *Catechism*.

The Tenth Commandment also requires us to banish envy from our hearts, reminding us that the devil's envy of God brought death into the world. Envy is defined as sadness in seeing another's goods, accompanied by the immediate desire to possess those goods.

Note: Our Lord placed being poor in spirit at the top of the list of His eight Beatitudes.

PART FOUR:

CHRISTIAN PRAYER

What Is Prayer?

Para. 2559–2562

What is prayer? The *Catechism* defines prayer simply as "the raising of one's mind and heart to God or the requesting of good things from God."

Humility is the foundation of prayer, says the *Catechism*, which poses the question: "When we pray, do we speak from the height of our pride and will, or 'out of the depths' of a humble and contrite heart? ... Only when we acknowledge that 'we do not know how to pray as we ought,' are we ready to receive freely the gift of prayer."

Saint Augustine points out that when we come to the well seeking water, Christ comes to meet us. He first seeks us and asks for a drink. His asking arises from God's desire for us. God's thirst encounters our thirst. He thirsts that we may thirst for Him.

Where does prayer come from? Scripture most frequently cites the heart. If the heart is far from God, the words of prayer are in vain.

The Universal Call to Prayer

Is there a universal call to prayer?

The *Catechism* tells us man is in search of God. God, in the act of creation, called every being into existence from nothingness. Even after man sinned and lost his likeness to God, he remained an image of his Creator and never lost his desire for the One who called him into existence.

All religions attest to man's essential search for God. The *Catechism* points out, however, that God calls us, first, to that mysterious encounter known as prayer. God always initiates. Man's first step in the process is to respond. Prayer is a reciprocal call.

Throughout the whole history of salvation, the covenant drama unfolds. The revelation of prayer in the Old Testament comes between the fall and the restoration of man.

"Prayer is bound up with human history," the *Catechism* states, "for it is the relationship with God in historical events."

Prayer in the Old Testament

Para. 2568–2573

Where is prayer revealed in the Bible? The *Catechism* says it comes between the fall and the restoration of man — between God's sorrowful call to our first parents, "Where are you? ... What have you done?" and the coming of His only Son into the world.

"Lo, I have come to do your will," says the Lord.

Prayer is intertwined with human history. Beginning with Abraham, the *Catechism* asserts, prayer is first revealed in the Old Testament. God calls Abraham in old age to leave Haran and travel to the land of Canaan, and Abraham, in faith, leaves the land of his ancestors. Then Abraham extends generous hospitality during a remarkable encounter with God at the oaks of Mamre, which foreshadows the annunciation of Christ, the Son of the promise.

Finally, Abraham offers his only son, Isaac, in sacrifice, and God, who will not spare His only Son, spares Abraham's.

King David and Prayer

Why is King David considered the king after God's own heart? According to the *Catechism*, it's because David was the "shepherd who prays for his people and prays in their name. His submission to the will of God, his praise, and his repentance will be a model for the prayer of the people."

When David prays the prayer of God's anointed, it is a faithful adherence to the divine promises and expresses a loving and joyful trust in God, the only King and Lord.

David is inspired by the Holy Spirit when he writes the psalms, and he becomes the first prophet of Jewish and Christian prayer. The prayer of Christ, the true Messiah and Son of David, will reveal and fulfill the meaning of this prayer.

Elijah, Father of Prophets

In the annals of prayer, why is Elijah such an important figure? Elijah is the "'father' of the prophets," the *Catechism* tells us.

The mission of the prophets was to educate the people of God so that they might experience conversion of the heart rather than merely participating in the ritual practices of religion. Saint James, in referring to Elijah, says, "The prayer of the righteous is powerful and effective." This is affirmed when Elijah asks God to restore the life of the son of a widow, and the Lord hears and answers Elijah's prayer.

On Mount Carmel, Elijah challenges 450 prophets of Baal to a prayer duel, before all the Israelites. Baal proves to be a false god, giving no answer to pleas from his prophets, while the God of Israel proves to be the true God by producing in response to Elijah's intercessory prayer a mighty fire to consume the holocaust.

The Psalms

Why are the Psalms such an important form of prayer?

The Psalms extend from the time of King David to the coming of the Messiah. They express both communal and individual prayer, evidencing a deepening in prayer for oneself and others.

The *Catechism* says the Psalms were gradually collected into five books known as the Psalter or Praises. They are considered the "masterwork of prayer" in the Old Testament.

The Psalms both commemorate the promises God has kept and anticipate the Messiah who will fulfill them definitively. Jesus both prayed the Psalms and fulfilled them. The Psalms remain essential to the prayer of the Church.

Jesus Prays

Para. 2598–2601

Where is the drama of prayer fully revealed? The *Catechism* tells us it is first revealed to us by observing Jesus Christ, the Word of God, in prayer — then by hearing how He teaches us to pray, in order to realize how He hears our prayer.

Jesus learned to pray in His human heart under the guidance of His Mother. He learns the rhythms of the prayers of His people in the synagogue at Nazareth and the Temple in Jerusalem. But at the age of 12, He makes known that His prayer springs from an otherwise secret source: His relationship with God the Father.

For example, Jesus tells His earthly parents that He must be about His heavenly Father's business. Luke's Gospel emphasizes that, before all the decisive moments of Jesus' mission — His Baptism, His Transfiguration, His Passion — He prays, humbly committing His will to His Father's.

The Master of Prayer

Para. 2599–2606

How did the apostles learn to pray? By observing their Leader, the Master of prayer: Jesus Christ.

The *Catechism* reminds us that Jesus often drew apart, frequently at night on a mountaintop, to pray in solitude. He includes everyone in His prayer, for He has taken on humanity in His Incarnation, and He offers us all to the Father when He offers Himself.

By His human prayer, the Word who has become flesh shares in all that His "brethren" experience. He sympathizes with our weakness in order to free us.

Thanksgiving precedes Jesus' prayer, as in the raising of Lazarus from the dead. Before the miracle, Jesus prays, "Father, I thank you for having heard me," which implies that the Father always hears His petitions. It implies, too, that Jesus continually made petitions.

Jesus also reveals how to ask: Say thank you before the gift is given.

Jesus' Unique Priestly Prayer

Para. 2604–2606

How is the priestly prayer of Jesus unique in the economy of salvation? According to the *Catechism*, it is unique because it reveals the ever-present prayer of Jesus and, at the same time, contains what Jesus teaches us about our prayer to Our Father.

As Jesus fulfills His Father's plan of love, He gives us a glimpse of the depth of His filial prayer when He agonizes in the Garden, "Abba, not my will, but thine." His last words on the Cross exhibit prayer and gift of self when He says, "Father, forgive them for they know not what they do." Later, with a loud cry, He surrenders His spirit.

"All the troubles, for all time," states the *Catechism*, "of humanity enslaved by sin and death, all the petitions and intercessions of salvation history are summed up in this cry of the incarnate Word ... who became the source of eternal salvation to all who obey him."

When Does Jesus Teach Us to Pray?

Para. 2607

According to the *Catechism*, whenever Jesus prays, He is teaching us how to pray. His prayer to His Father is the path of faith, hope, and charity to God.

In the Gospels, however, Jesus also gives us His explicit teaching on prayer, leading us wisely and progressively from where we are toward the Father.

Jesus used this approach with the crowds who were following Him, building on what they already knew from the old Covenant, opening them to the newness of the coming Kingdom, renewing this newness in parables, and finally speaking openly of the Father to His disciples who will teach prayer in His Church.

Filial Boldness

What does the *Catechism* mean when it says, Jesus teaches us to pray with "*filial boldness*"? Filial boldness means praying like the son or daughter that we are.

"Whatever you ask in prayer, believe that you will receive it and you will," Jesus says. The key is the faith that does not doubt. Jesus was disheartened by His neighbors and His own disciples' lack of faith. He greatly admired the great faith exhibited by the Roman centurion and the Canaanite woman.

Of what does the prayer of faith consist? It contains the disposition of heart to do the will of the Father — a concern for cooperating with the divine plan. In Jesus, the Kingdom of God is at hand.

In addition to conversion and faith, Jesus calls us to watchfulness — attentive to Him Who is and Him Who comes — in memory of His first coming in the flesh and in hopefulness of His second coming in glory.

Three Parables about Prayer

Para. 2613

What are the three parables that Jesus tells about prayer in St. Luke's Gospel?

The first is what the *Catechism* calls "the importunate friend." This is the friend who wakes a pal at midnight in order to borrow three loaves of bread to feed a visitor.

The second parable is "the importunate widow" who persistently pleads for her rights from a reluctant judge until the wearied judge rules in her favor. This parable illustrates the need to pray always and with the patience of faith. Jesus closes this parable with the poignant question, "When the Son of Man comes, will He find any faith on the earth?"

The third parable centers on the Pharisee and the tax collector, commending the tax collector for his humility because he asks God, "Be merciful to me, a sinner," a prayer that the Church adopts as its own when we pray, "Lord have mercy" during the Mass.

Jesus Always Answers Our Prayers

Does Jesus always answer our prayers? The *Catechism* says yes. Jesus always answers prayers offered in faith; He said, "Your faith has made you well. Go in peace."

The *Catechism* cites three examples where Jesus reacts to different kinds of prayer of faith: the leper, the Canaanite woman, and the good thief. The prayer of petition is exhibited in the actions of the bearers of the paralyzed man and the hemorrhaging woman who is healed by merely touching Jesus' cloak.

Finally, urgent prayer is heard from the lips of the blind men: "Have mercy on us, Son of David." This is remembered today as the "Jesus prayer": "Lord, Jesus Christ, Son of God, have mercy on me, a sinner!" Saint Augustine parses this prayer thus: "Jesus prays for us as our priest, prays in us as our Head, and is prayed to by us as our God."

Prayer in the Early Church

How did the first community of believers in Jerusalem pray?

The *Catechism* tells us that as Christ's disciples were gathered together on the first Pentecost, the Spirit of the Promise was poured out on them. They were in one place, devoting themselves to prayer. The Holy Spirit came to teach the Church; to recall for her everything Jesus said and to form her in a life of prayer.

"In the first community of Jerusalem," the *Catechism* states, "believers 'devoted themselves to the apostles' teaching and fellowship, to the breaking of the bread, and prayers.'"

This sequence is characteristic of Church worship founded on apostolic faith, lived in charity, and nourished by the Eucharist. The faithful hear these prayers and read them in the Scriptures and make them their own, particularly the Psalms.

Thus, the Holy Spirit keeps the memory of Jesus Christ alive in His Church at prayer. He leads her to the fullness of truth. He also inspires to express the unfathomable mystery of Christ at work in His Church.

Blessing and Adoration

Para. 2626–2628

When we speak of blessing in prayer, what exactly do we mean?

The *Catechism* defines blessing as a basic movement of Christian prayer, an encounter between God and man. God's gift and man's acceptance of that gift are united in dialogue with each other. God blesses, and the human heart can respond to bless the One who is the source of every blessing.

The *Catechism* states that two fundamental forms express this movement. Human prayer ascends in the Holy Spirit through Christ *to* the Father, and it implores the grace of the Holy Spirit that descends through Christ *from* the Father.

Adoration, says the *Catechism*, is man's first attitude, acknowledging that he is a creature before his Creator. "It exalts the greatness of the Lord who made us and the almighty power of the Savior who sets us free from evil," notes the *Catechism*. "Adoration is homage of the spirit to the 'King of Glory.' ... Adoration of the thrice-holy and sovereign God of love blends with humility and gives assurance to our supplications."

Prayer of Petition

Para. 2629–2633

What is the most spontaneous form of prayer? The *Catechism* says it is the prayer of petition. Through prayer of petition, we express our awareness of our true relationship with God.

We are not creatures of our own making. We did not begin ourselves, nor will we end ourselves. We are not the masters of adversity. We are sinners who know we have turned away from God. Our prayer of petition is already a turning back to Him. In the Risen Christ, the Church's petition is buoyed by hope.

The first movement in the prayer of petition is asking for forgiveness. That is, says the *Catechism*, "a prerequisite for righteous and pure prayer." In the hierarchy of petitions, we pray for the Kingdom, then what is necessary to welcome and cooperate with its coming.

When we share in God's saving love, we understand that every need can become the object of petition. Christ is glorified by what we ask the Father in His name.

Intercessory Prayer

Para. 2634–2636

What do we mean by intercessory prayer? The *Catechism* defines it as "asking on behalf of another ... characteristic of a heart attuned to God's mercy." It is a prayer of petition that leads us to pray as Jesus did.

Jesus is the one Intercessor with the Father on behalf of all men, especially sinners, because, says the *Catechism*, Jesus "is able for all time to save those who draw near to God through him, since he always lives to make intercession for them."

When one prays intercessory prayer, he or she is looking out not just for one's own interests but for the interests of others, even for one's enemies. The intercession of Christians recognizes no boundaries, says the *Catechism*. Prayers are extended for all men, for kings or for persecutors, and even for the salvation of those who reject the Gospel.

Prayers of Thanksgiving,
Prayers of Praise

Para. 2639–2643

How best to thank God? The *Catechism* tells us that every event and need can become an offering of thanksgiving. Saint Paul often begins his letters with thanksgiving. And the Lord Jesus is always part of such a prayer.

In the First Letter to Timothy, Paul writes, "Give thanks in all circumstances, for this is the will of God in Christ Jesus for you." The *Catechism* says that it is the form of prayer that most immediately recognizes God is God. It praises God, not just for what He has done, but simply for who He is. "Praise embraces the other forms of prayer and carries them toward him who is its source and goal: the 'one God, the Father, from whom are all things and for whom we exist.'"

The sacrifice of praise is the Eucharist. It is, the *Catechism* notes, "'the pure offering' of the whole Body of Christ to the glory of God's name."

The Will to Pray

What are the important elements to prayer? "In order to pray," says the *Catechism*, "one must have the will to pray." It is not enough to know what Scripture reveals about prayer — we must learn *how* to pray.

Through sacred tradition, in a believing and praying Church, the Holy Spirit teaches the children of God how to pray. The *Catechism* tells us that prayer is one of the several wellsprings where Christ awaits us to enable us to drink of the Holy Spirit.

The Church exhorts all the faithful to acquire a surpassing knowledge of Christ through the reading of Divine Scripture. Prayer should always accompany such reading in order that a dialogue may take place between God and man. We speak to Him when we pray. He speaks to us when we read the Divine Oracles.

The spiritual writers say, notes the *Catechism*, "Seek in reading and you will find in meditating; knock in mental prayer and it will be opened to you by contemplation."

Prayer with the Theological Virtues

Para. 2656–2660

How do the three theological virtues — faith, hope, and charity — fit into our prayer? The *Catechism* says, "One enters into prayer as one enters into liturgy: by the narrow gate of *faith*. ... It is the Face of the Lord that we seek and desire; it is his Word that we want to hear and keep."

The Holy Spirit instructs us to celebrate the liturgy in expectation of Jesus' return, and teaches us to pray in hope. Hope is nourished in us by the prayer of the Church and personal prayer. The Psalms, especially through their concrete and varied language, teach us to fix our hope in God.

Love is poured into our hearts by the Holy Spirit. Prayer, formed by the liturgical life, draws everything into Christ's love for us, which enables us to respond to Him by loving as He loved us.

Love is the source of prayer.

When Should We Pray?

When should we pray? The *Catechism* asserts that anytime is the right time.

We learn to pray by hearing the Word of God and sharing in His Paschal Mystery. But the Holy Spirit "is offered to us at all times, in the events of *each day*, to make prayer spring up from us." Jesus teaches us that, like providence, time is in the Father's hands. We encounter Him in the present. Not yesterday. Not tomorrow. Today.

Psalm 95 cautions, "If today, you hear His voice, harden not your hearts." Praying through the events of the day is one of the secrets of the Kingdom as revealed to little children, the faithful, and the poor of the Beatitudes. This means that the coming of the Kingdom can influence the march of history as well as humble, everyday events.

Way of Prayer

What do we mean by the "Way of Prayer"?

The *Catechism* tells us that, in the living tradition of prayer, each Church proposes to her members a language for prayer within the context of its historical, cultural, and social background. The Magisterium of the Catholic Church has the task of discerning if these ways of praying are faithful to the traditions of the apostolic faith.

There is, the *Catechism* insists, "no other way of Christian prayer than Christ." Why? "Whether our prayer is communal or personal, vocal or interior, it has access to the Father only if we pray 'in the name' of Jesus," which means, "God saves."

It is through His sacred humanity that the Holy Spirit teaches us to pray to our Father.

Power of the Name of Jesus

Para. 2665–2669

Why is the calling on the Name of Jesus so powerful? According to the *Catechism*, "To pray 'Jesus' is to invoke him and to call him within us." We are welcoming the Son of God who loved us and gave Himself up for us.

A simple invocation developed through tradition in both East and West and transmitted by the spiritual writers of the Sinai, Syria, and Mount Athos is, "Lord Jesus Christ, Son of God, have mercy on us sinners." Through this prayer, the human heart is opened to human wretchedness and the Savior's mercy.

Invoking the Holy Name of Jesus is the simplest way of praying always. If the heart is humbly attentive, the prayer is not lost by heaping up empty phrases. It holds fast to the Word and brings forth fruit with patience.

The prayer of the Church also honors the heart of Jesus and the Way of the Cross, which we call "making the Stations." Making the Stations follows Jesus from the Praetorium to Golgotha and to the tomb.

The Holy Spirit and Prayer

Whom do we most need in order to say, "Jesus is Lord"? The Holy Spirit.

The *Catechism* says that every time we invoke Jesus, it is the Holy Spirit who draws us onto the path of prayer. And since it is the Holy Spirit who teaches us to pray by recalling Jesus, how can we not pray to the Holy Spirit, too?

"The Church invites us to call upon the Holy Spirit every day, especially at the beginning and the end of every important action," the *Catechism* says. And how should we pray to Him? The traditional form is to invoke the Father through Christ our Lord to give us the Consoler, the Spirit. The most direct prayer, counsels the *Catechism,* is, simply, "Come Holy Spirit," to which the words, "fill the hearts of your faithful, enkindle in them the fire of your love," are frequently added.

The Holy Spirit is the artisan of the living tradition of prayer and the Master of interior prayer.

The Hail Mary

What is the meaning of the "Hail Mary prayer"? There are multiple meanings, explains the *Catechism*.

When we say "Hail Mary" or "Rejoice, Mary," we are repeating the greeting of the angel Gabriel to Mary at the Annunciation. It is God who actually greets Mary through His intermediary, Gabriel.

The next phrase, "Full of grace, the Lord is with you," asserts that Mary is full of grace because the source of grace — the Lord — is with her.

"Blessed art thou among women and blessed is the fruit of your womb," echoes Elizabeth greeting her young cousin who has come to assist her during her delivery of John the Baptist.

"Holy Mary, Mother of God" means that because Mary gives us Jesus, her Son, the God-Man, Mary is the Mother of God and our Mother.

The final plea to Mary, "Pray for us sinners, now and at the hour of our death," acknowledges that we are sinners, now, hoping that Mary can welcome us as our Mother at the hour we die and lead us to her Son, Jesus, in Paradise.

A Cloud of Witnesses

Like the Saints, do our loved ones who have gone before us still participate in the living tradition of prayer? The *Catechism* says they participate by the witness of their lives, the transmission of their writings, and their actual prayer right now.

Witnesses in Heaven contemplate God, praise Him, and "constantly care for those whom they have left on earth." When Saints enter into the joy of their Master, they are "put in charge of many things." The *Catechism* asserts that the Saints' intercession is "their most exalted service to God's plan." Thus, we should be asking them to intercede for us and for the entire world.

Sometimes personal charisms of witnesses to God's love for mankind are passed on, as the spirit of Elijah was passed on to Elisha and John the Baptist in order that their followers may have a share in their spirit.

The rich diversity of the different schools of spirituality are refractions of the one pure light of the Holy Spirit.

Where are the servants of prayer? The Christian family is the first place of education in prayer, says the *Catechism*. The family is the "Domestic Church" where children learn to pray and to persevere in prayer.

Ordained ministers are also responsible for forming their brothers and sisters in prayer. Many in the religious life have consecrated their whole lives to prayer. The consecrated life is sustained by prayer, and is one of the living sources of contemplation and spiritual life of the Church.

Catechesis aims to teach all members of the Church to meditate on the Word of God in personal and liturgical prayer, internalizing it in order to bear fruit in a new life. Prayer groups and spiritual direction can also be powerful tools in the practice of prayer.

The Life of Prayer
Para. 2697–2699

What is the life of our heart? The *Catechism* answers, "Prayer is the life of the new heart. It ought to animate us at every moment." But we tend to forget the One who is our all.

The Fathers of the spiritual life in the Deuteronomic and prophetic traditions, the *Catechism* notes, say that "prayer is a remembrance of God often awakened by the memory of the heart: 'We must remember God more often than we draw breath.'"

We cannot, however, pray at all times if we have not learned to pray at specific times. The tradition of the Church proposes Morning and Evening Prayer, grace before and after meals, the Liturgy of the Hours, Sundays centered on the Eucharist, and the cycle of the liturgical year with its great feasts as the basic rhythms of the Christian's life of prayer.

There are three major expressions of prayer: vocal, meditative, and contemplative. The Lord leads all on paths pleasing to Him, and the believer responds according to the disposition of his heart.

Expressions of Prayer

How best to express ourselves to God? Our prayer takes flesh, says the *Catechism*, when we use mental or vocal words to talk to God, who speaks to us through His Word.

Our heart must be involved in prayer. We must be present to Him Whom we are addressing. "Whether or not our prayer is heard depends not on the number of our words," says St. John Chrysostom, "but on the fervor of our souls."

Vocal prayer is essential to the Christian life. Jesus taught the perfect vocal prayer — the Our Father — to His disciples. He prayed aloud the liturgical prayers in the synagogue. He also prayed aloud personally, exultantly praising the Father as well as expressing His agony in Gethsemane.

Vocal prayer fits the needs of our human nature. We are body and spirit, and this need corresponds to a divine requirement. God seeks worshipers in truth and spirit.

Meditative Prayer

What is "meditative prayer"? The *Catechism* defines meditative prayer as, above all, a quest.

The mind seeks to understand the why and how of the Christian life in order to adhere and respond to what the Lord is asking. Since the required attentiveness is difficult to sustain, we are aided by books, such as Sacred Scripture (especially the Gospels), holy icons, liturgical texts of the day or season, and writings of the Spiritual Fathers.

If we meditate on what we read, we make it our own. If we are humble and faithful in meditation, we discover in meditation the movements that stir the heart, enabling us to discern those movements. We are asking, "Lord, what do you want me to do?"

The *Catechism* urges us to develop the desire to meditate regularly. All meditation should advance us to the knowledge of the love of the Lord Jesus.

The Prayer of the Hour of Jesus
Para. 2746–2751

The "Prayer of the Hour of Jesus" is an extraordinary prayer, states the *Catechism*. It is the longest prayer recorded in the Gospels that Jesus offers to His Father. He prays it as He is facing the hour of His Passion.

The *Catechism* claims the prayer "embraces the whole economy of creation and salvation as well as [Jesus'] death and Resurrection. The prayer ... always remains his own, just as his Passover 'once for all' remains ever present in the liturgy of his Church."

In this paschal and sacrificial prayer, also known as Jesus' priestly prayer, everything is concisely reviewed and summarized in Christ: God and the world, the Word and the flesh, eternal life and time, the love that hands itself over, and the sin that betrays it. Jesus fulfilled the work of the Father completely.

His prayer, like His sacrifice, extends until the end of time.

The Battle of Prayer

Why is prayer a battle? Prayer is both a gift of grace and a determined response on our part, the *Catechism* tells us. It takes effort.

Who is the battle against? Against ourselves and against the devil who does all he can to turn us away from prayer and God and union with Him. If we do not live habitually according to the Spirit of Christ, we cannot pray habitually in his name.

"We pray as we live," says the *Catechism*, and "we live as we pray."

One of the most universal difficulties in prayer is distraction. The simple and most effective answer to distraction is to turn back to our heart, for distraction reveals to what we are attached. This humble awareness can prompt us to offer our hearts to the Lord for purification.

Perfect Prayer

Para. 2761–2763

What is the perfect prayer? The prayer that was taught us by the Lord Jesus Himself: the Our Father.

The *Catechism* cites the Our Father as "truly the summary of the whole gospel." Saint Augustine writes, "Run through all the words of the holy prayers [in Scripture], and I do not think you will find anything in them that is not contained and included in the Lord's Prayer."

All the Scriptures — the Law, the Prophets, and the Psalms — "are fulfilled in Christ," says the *Catechism*. This is the Good News of the Gospel.

Saint Thomas Aquinas gives equally high praise to the Our Father. "The Lord's Prayer," he says, "is the most perfect of prayers. ... In it, we ask, not only for all the things we can rightly desire, but also in the sequence that they should be desired."

The rightness of our life in Jesus will depend on the rightness of our prayer.

Why the "Lord's Prayer"?

Para. 2765–2766

What does the Lord's Prayer — *"oratio Dominica"* — mean? It refers to a prayer that is, according to the *Catechism,* "truly unique" as it is "of the Lord."

As the only Son of God the Father, Jesus, in speaking the words His Father gave Him, is the Master of our prayer. In addition, as Word Incarnate, Jesus, in His human heart, knows the needs of His human brothers and sisters. In revealing them to us, He is also the "model of our prayer."

Jesus, however, does not merely give us a formula to repeat mechanically. Jesus not only gives the words of the "Our Father," He gives us the Spirit by Whom the words become in us "spirit and life." The prayer to Our Father, the *Catechism* asserts, "is inserted into the mysterious mission of the Son and of the Spirit."

Meaning of the "Our"
in "Our Father"

Para. 2786–2793

What are we expressing when we use the word "our" in relation to God?

The *Catechism* tells us the adjective "our" does not mean possession, but an entirely new relationship with God. It means that we recognize that all God's promises of love coming through the Prophets are fulfilled in the new and eternal covenant in His Christ. We have become His people, and He is our God.

We are to respond to this gift in Jesus Christ with love and faithfulness. The Church is this new communion of God and man.

"In praying 'our' Father,'" the *Catechism* states, "each of the baptized is praying in this communion: 'The company of those who believed were of one heart and soul'" (Acts 4:32).

But the "our" in the Our Father, if prayed sincerely, also includes all for whom God gave His beloved Son, revealing the dimensions of God's love for all, even those who do not yet know Him.

Calling God "Our Father"

Para. 2786–2796

How can we — mere mortals that we are — call God our Father? The *Catechism* says we can do this because His Son, who became Man, has revealed the Father to us, and because His Spirit makes Him known to us.

When we pray to the Father, we are in communion with Him and with His Son, Jesus Christ. We come to know and recognize Him with an ever-new sense of wonder.

The first phase of the Our Father is a blessing and adoration before it is a supplication. We can adore the Father because He has caused us to be reborn to His life by adopting us through Baptism. He incorporates us into the Body of His Christ. The free gift of adoption requires conversion on our part.

Praying to our Father should develop in us two fundamental dispositions: first, the desire to become like God by responding to His grace; and second, a humble and trusting heart that enables us to become like children, because it is to little children that the Father is revealed.

Who Art in Heaven

Para. 2794–2796

When we refer to "Our Father, who art in Heaven," are we talking to a God who is far removed from us?

On the contrary, says the *Catechism*. We are talking to a Father who is close to humble and contrite hearts. We assert that God is in the hearts of the just, as He is in His Holy Temple. He is in Heaven, His dwelling place; the Father's house is our homeland. Sin has exiled us, but conversion of heart enables us to return to the Father, to Heaven.

"[Christians] are in the flesh," the *Catechism* states, "but they do not live according to the flesh. They spend their lives on earth, but are citizens of heaven."

Hallowed Be Thy Name

Para. 2807–2815

What do we mean when we say to the Father, "hallowed be thy Name"? We are recognizing the holiness of God.

The *Catechism* tells us that "the holiness of God is the inaccessible center of his eternal mystery. What is revealed of it in creation and history, Scripture calls 'glory,' the radiance of his majesty."

When God made man in His image and likeness, He crowned man with glory and honor, but when man sinned, he fell short of the glory of God. From that time on, God manifested His holiness by revealing and giving His Name, beginning with Moses, in order to restore man to the image of his Creator.

Finally, in the person of Jesus, God's Holy Name is given to us in the Flesh as "Savior." He reveals this through His Word and through His Sacrifice. At the end of Jesus' Passover, the Father gives to the Son the name that is above all names: "Jesus Christ is Lord, to the Glory of the Father."

Thy Kingdom Come

Para. 2816–2821

What are we asking God the Father when, in the Lord's Prayer, we plead, "Thy Kingdom come"? The *Catechism* states, "The Kingdom of God lies ahead of us. It is brought near in the Word incarnate [Jesus Christ], it is proclaimed throughout the whole Gospel, and it has come in Christ's death and Resurrection." In the Eucharist, it is actually in our midst.

When Christ hands the Kingdom over to the Father, the Kingdom will come in glory. Saint Cyprian speculates that the Kingdom of God may even mean Christ Himself coming into our lives. In the context of the Lord's Prayer, "Thy Kingdom come" refers primarily to the final coming of the reign of God through Christ's return.

Since Pentecost, the coming of God's reign is the work of the Holy Spirit. The Kingdom of God is righteousness and peace and joy in the Holy Spirit. The end times in which we are living is the age of the outpouring of the Holy Spirit and a decisive battle between "the flesh and the Spirit."

Thy Will Be Done

Para. 2822–2827

When we say, "Thy Will be done, on earth as it is in Heaven," what are we asking of our Father? The *Catechism* explains that God desires that all men be saved and come to know the Truth. He does not wish anyone to perish.

In His Son, Jesus Christ, and through His human will, the will of the Father has been perfectly fulfilled once for all. The Lord made this clear on entering His public ministry: "I have come to do your will, O God."

Only Jesus can say, "I always do what is pleasing to Him," even unto death as He prayed in the Garden of Gethsemane, "Not my will, but yours be done." Thus we ask our Father to unite our will to His Son's in order to fulfill the Father's will.

By prayer, we can discern God's will and receive the endurance to carry it out. Jesus taught that one enters the Kingdom of God not by speaking only words but by doing the will of His Father in Heaven.

Give Us This Day Our Daily Bread

Para. 2828–2837

When we ask Our Father to "give us this day our daily bread," are we merely asking for daily nourishment?

We are, says the *Catechism*: "The Father who gives us life cannot but give us the nourishment life requires — all appropriate goods and blessings, both material and spiritual." And much more: to those who seek the Kingdom of God and its righteousness, God has promised to give all else besides.

Since everything belongs to God, he who possesses God possesses everything, if he himself is not found wanting before God.

The drama of hunger in the world, therefore, calls upon all Christians to exercise responsibility toward their needy brethren both in their behavior and in their solidarity with the human family. It also applies to another hunger: thirst for the Word of the Lord and for Catholics, receiving His Body in the Eucharist which is, indeed, our daily Bread.

Forgive Us Our Trespasses

Para. 2839–2843

What is the most daunting petition in the Lord's Prayer? The *Catechism* says it is when we ask God our Father to forgive our sins as we forgive others, meaning that if we do not forgive those who have sinned against us, we don't expect the Father to forgive us.

God's outpouring of mercy "cannot penetrate our hearts as long as we have not forgiven those who have trespassed against us," the *Catechism* states. This is sobering.

The *Catechism* adds there has to be a vital participation, coming from the depths of the heart, in the holiness and the mercy and the love of God. Only the Holy Spirit can make our mind the same as the mind of Jesus Christ, who could forgive even those who crucified Him.

The heart that offers itself to the Holy Spirit can turn injury into compassion, purifying the memory so as to transform the hurt into intercession. Forgiveness bears witness to the world that love is stronger than hate.

Lead Us Not into Temptation

Para. 2846–2849

What do we mean when we ask our Heavenly Father not to lead us into temptation? Is it possible for God to tempt us? It is not, asserts the *Catechism*: "God cannot be tempted by evil and he himself tempts no one."

Translating from the Greek verb "to lead" into a single English verb is the difficulty. The Greek verb means we are asking God not to allow us to take the way that leads us to sin. This petition addresses the battle between flesh and the spirit, imploring the Spirit of discernment and truth.

With the Holy Spirit, we can discern between trials that are necessary for our growth and temptations that lead to sin and death. Discernment also entails distinguishing between being tempted and consenting to temptation. It unmasks the lie of temptation that makes the object look desirable when, in fact, its fruit is death.

God will never allow us to be tempted beyond our strength, says St. Paul. The battle, however, can only be won by prayer.

Deliver Us from Evil

When we ask God our Father to deliver us from evil, are we referring to an idea or a person?

We are not referring to an abstraction, says the *Catechism*. We are referring to a person — the evil one, Satan, the fallen angel who throws himself across God's plan of salvation accomplished in Christ. Jesus labeled Satan a murderer, a liar, and the father of lies.

We do not pray alone. We pray in communion with the Church for the whole human family. Our interdependence in the drama of sin and death is turned into solidarity in the Body of Christ, the Communion of Saints.

If one entrusts himself to God, one does not dread the devil. Victory over Satan, the prince of the world, was attained once and for all when Jesus freely gave Himself over to death in order to give us His life.

AFTERWORD

Life in Christ. Christ in Life.

The *Catechism* says Christ's whole life is mystery. No part more mysterious than the "hidden" years, the 30 years when Jesus lived as a private citizen, so to speak, before He became the Public Man.

The *Catechism* also tells us He was never not on His redemptive mission. From the "cradle to the Cross" He was modeling the perfect life, first for his parents, then his peers. He grew up with them as a baby, a young boy, and a teenager in His father's workshop before He advanced to the Man/Preacher/Teacher who changed the world.

We have no photographs of Him, lest you count the Shroud of Turin, and even then we must stretch our imagination.

"Keep your eyes on Jesus," we are frequently admonished. To do that we need to think creatively.

I have come to postulate that Our Lord – who can appear as the gardener, a traveler on the road to Emmaus, or a beggar – presents Himself to each person in ways that draw us to Him. As an artist, I always hope to present Jesus in images that might bring the viewer closer to Our Lord. As I pondered the *Catechism*'s third Pillar, "Life in Christ," I began imagining "Christ in Life": those mysterious "hidden years." From those pictorial ruminations came these drawings which I share with you on the next page.

The Divine genius of the Eucharist today, 2,000 years hence, is that He is still among us. We no longer have to imagine Him. We can all recognize Him as one family in the "breaking of the bread."

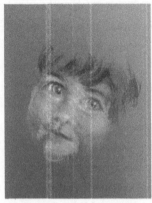

"And the Word became flesh ..." (Jn 1:14)

"Did you not know that I must be in my Father's house?" (Lk 2:49)

"The child grew and became strong, filled with wisdom; and the favor of God was upon him." (Lk 2:40)

"The Spirit of the Lord is upon me, because he has anointed me ..." (Lk 4:18; Is 61:1)

ABOUT THE AUTHOR

Peggy Stanton was the ABC Television network's first female news correspondent in Washington, DC, in 1966. Since 2012, she has used the reportorial skills acquired reporting the bad news on secular networks to report the Good News on Catholic networks, including Ave Maria Radio, where she has hosted several shows, including the "Order of Malta Minutes with the *Catechism*."

Peggy's columns and articles have appeared in numerous newspapers and magazines, including the *Washington Post*, the *Washington Times*, the *Saturday Evening Post*, the *News Leader* (Florida), and *Medjugorje* magazine. Her paintings have been exhibited in museums, churches, and art galleries.

Peggy is the author of *The Daniel Dilemma*, a book about the moral man in the public arena, and coauthor and illustrator of *How to Help Your Child Eat Right*, one of the earliest guides to better nutrition for children. Her memoir, *From the White House to the White Cross: Confessions of a TV News Correspondent*, was published in 2022 by Marian Press.

Peggy was the founder and president of a special events firm, Creative Solutions. The organization specialized in governmental, diplomatic, journalistic, and religious seminars in Washington, D.C. She was the founder and president of the Mary Anne Foundation, named after the mother and grandmother of the Prince of Peace, whose motto was "Peace through Love." The organization sponsored "Kids for Peace" activities for thousands of grade-school and high-school children in schools across the country, and participated in refugee missions during the Balkan war.

Peggy served as president of the Republican Congressional Wives Club, the International Neighbors Club, and the Nassau Republican Women's Club. She has been a board member of the Order of Malta American Association, Pregnancy Aid, and the Ivy Foundation, and currently serves on the Order of Malta Dental-Medical Clinic board.

A Dame of Malta, Peggy is the widow of deceased former Congressman Bill Stanton, the mother of Kelly Fordon, and the grandmother of Jack, Charlie, Megan and Peter Fordon. She lives in Grosse Pointe, Michigan.